PLATTELAND

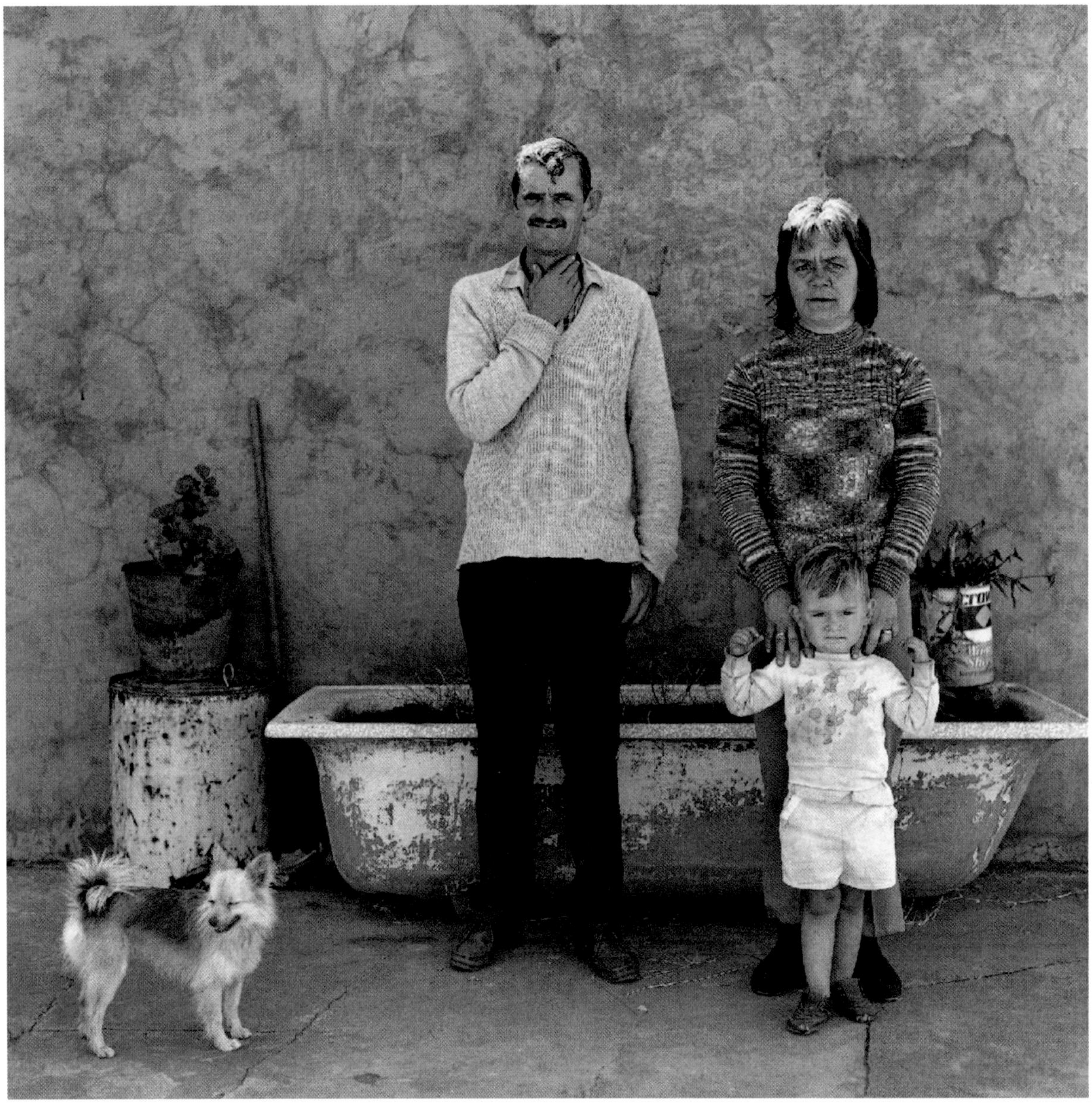

Jan Venter, diamond digger, with wife and son, Western Transvaal, 1986

To Lynda, my wife, who has lovingly supported me in my commitment to this project. Her deep insight into my vision has helped me clarify image and text. Her fine aesthetic sensibility pervades this book.

To Paul and Amanda, my children, whose creative imaginations, joy in exploring and innocent perception of truth are my constant inspiration.

To them I dedicate this book.

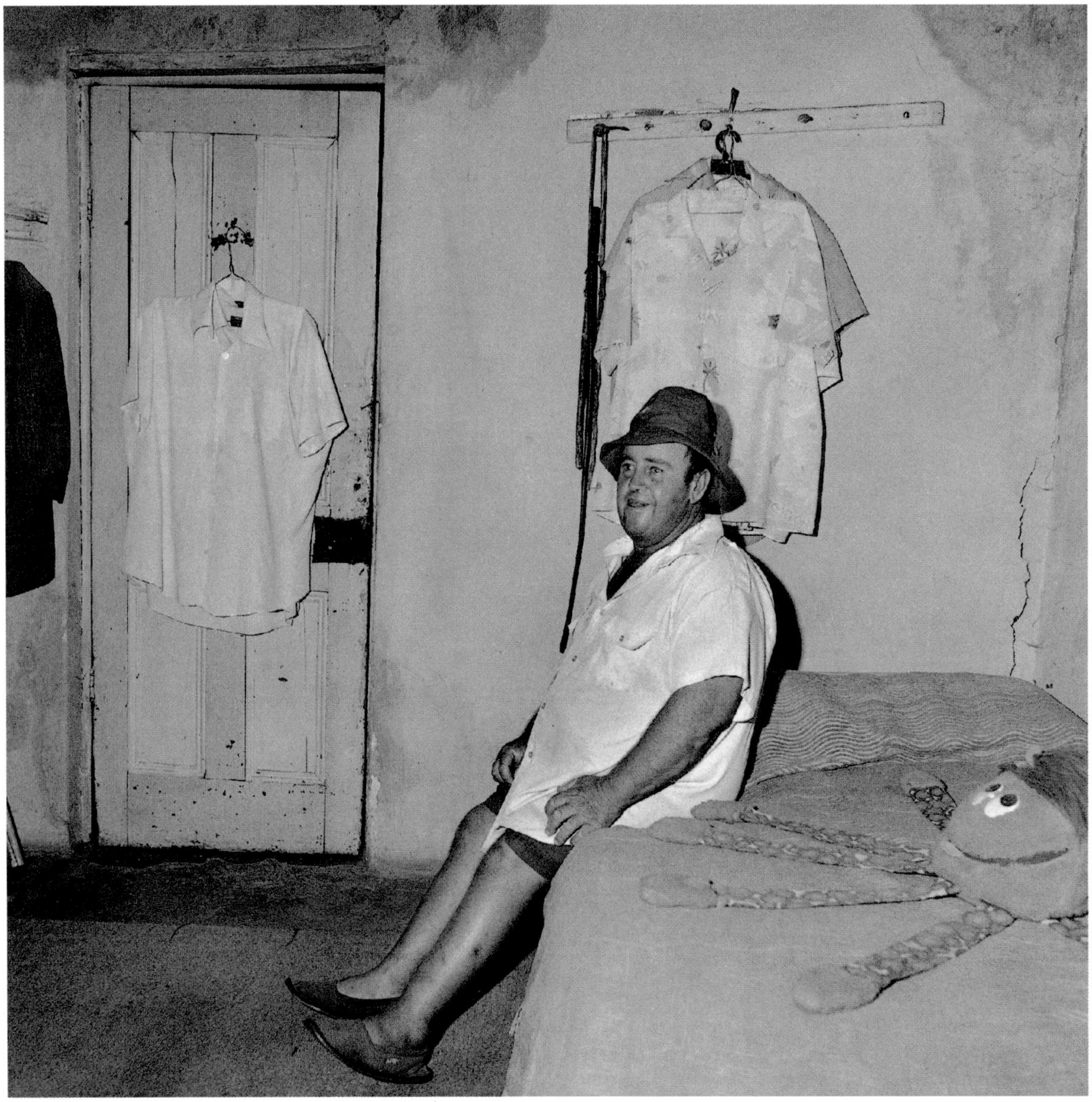

Boetie Nel, grape farmer, Northern Cape, 1992

PLATTELAND

IMAGES FROM RURAL SOUTH AFRICA

ROGER BALLEN

St. Martin's Press
New York

Book design: Beith Process, Johannesburg

ISBN 0-312-14187-4

First published in South Africa by William Waterman Publications

First U.S. Edition
10 9 8 7 6 5 4 3 2 1

National Book Printers
Drukkery Street
Goodwood, Western Cape

ACKNOWLEDGEMENTS

I want to thank the following people who made this book possible:

Dennis da Silva, my friend, whose enthusiastic commitment to my work and whose generosity of spirit go far beyond the realm of our professional relationship. His skills in the craft of printing and reproduction and his vigilant standards of excellence have been essential to the qualitative production of this book.

Dot Zylstra, Jim Smith, Jeremy Wightman, Brian Altshuler, Sharon Delano who assisted in the refinement of text and image.

Werner Bothner and Keith Brewerton whose technical expertise so clearly expresses itself throughout the photographic images.

Ebineezer, Leroy, and Oliver who always keep me in touch with the primeval forces of life.

My father Irving and sisters Kate and Sian in New York who share my excitement for the black and white photograph.

Those individuals whom I have photographed whose lives have become part of mine and whose trust and friendship I will always value.

Platteland is literally translated from the Afrikaans as 'flatlands' and refers to the South African countryside. The term implies more than a description of its geographic character, its expansive, often brutal, monotonous landscape. It connotes a particular state of mind.

To the eye of the photographer the visual qualities of this place are striking: there is an emptiness, a barrenness, an expansiveness that is almost surreal; a strangeness of light, an other-worldliness. So, too, is its psyche.

From the early seventies when I first frequented these parts, circumstances brought me intimately into the life of the platteland. Tentatively at first, and then with purpose, I began a photographic journey which became a search for aesthetic symbols that synthesized an essential character of this place, its historical presence, its mythology.

For years I have been fascinated by the faded and crumbling glory of the 'dorps' with their decrepit portents of grandeur and remnants of unfulfilled promises. Initially it was by chance, and then it was by choice, that I entered this world. My fascination with this circumstance of people and place came from a deep sense that what I was encountering, the visual dramas I was witnessing, were more significant than the events themselves; that in these ordinary towns and everyday happenings there abounded an elusive quality that, distilled into the photographic image, would reveal an essential aspect of the tragedy that pervades this troubled land.

Fundamentally, what drew me to this subject was the profound irony that, despite half a century of political privilege, here in the physical heart of White South Africa, even in a system created to secure their survival, were archetypes of alienation and immobility, victims of both political forces and personal circumstances, defending themselves against economic deprivation and psychological anguish in a hostile and unyielding environment.

On abandoned farms, on the outskirts of towns, next to worked-out mines I met protagonists in this drama. Some lived a nomadic existence drifting from place to place finding work haphazardly, others leased plots on which to grow maize or potatoes. Some were diamond diggers hoping for a 'stroke of luck', some were traders who filled their trucks with subsistence goods bought from Asian shops to sell in tribal areas, others were railway workers whose escapades had taken them deep into Africa.

There prevailed a perceived glory of a past heritage, its folklore and myth handed down by word of mouth from parents and grandparents, a reference back to ancestors who, as pioneers over a century ago, had crossed the African frontier, hunted game and tamed 'savages'. Those were remembered as the days of the mass migrations of springbok, zebra and wildebeest. Education came through the veld and Bible. Land in 'the good old days' was free, and there was mutual respect amongst all races. A man could kick the earth and become wealthy; wherever one went there were diamonds and gold.

This legendary land has ceased to be. Paradoxically, the people I encountered were surviving hand-to-mouth existences. Many South African rural areas are faced with a crisis of economic disorientation and decline. Jobs for unskilled people have become increasingly scarce, and those who seek work have to show a marked ingenuity or be prepared to accept poor working conditions and low wages. Menial jobs such as fixing cars and machinery, selling vegetables on the roadside, peddling second-hand goods or collecting recyclable paper and cans have become increasingly widespread. A fatalistic impotence has taken over.

The tenuous economic circumstances that prevail are evident in the conditions of the homes that I encountered. Houses are rented cheaply or are traditional, old family homes. Decay and dilapidation are everywhere. Building maintenance is postponed and warped floors, cracked ceilings, peeling paint, exposed electrical wires and broken plumbing are common. Old car batteries are used to power light bulbs and TV sets, plastic sheets cover broken window panes, and when pumps break, hand pumps draw up underground water from wells. Heat for cooking is often obtained from obsolete coal-burning stoves. Ignorance, dejection, apathy and a lack of ambition result in unsanitary conditions. There is an all-pervading smell of filth. Many homes smell distinctly of unwashed clothes, and bed linen. Pests are uncontrolled except, on occasion, by brown sticky paper dangling from above and copper wire mouse traps lurking in dark corners. Basic provisions: white bread, salt, tea, sugar, 'Coke', matches and candles are staples in kitchens that smell of stale cooking oil and paraffin. Mealie meal, cooked in large quantities, stands around for long periods in a pot on the stove, to be eaten with fatty meat cooked on an outdoor fire.

Homes contain furniture inherited from family members or acquired second-hand and a 'make-do' attitude is apparent. Faded, perished and stained upholstery and curtains, threadbare carpets, chipped and splintered timber are conspicuous. Beds lack springs and sag in the centre, sometimes laden with unironed, crumpled laundry. Handwork in the form of embroidered or crocheted cushions, doilies and antimacassars are proudly displayed as mementoes from anniversary celebrations. Birthday and Christmas cards, dried flower arrangements, and glass and china objects, considered to be precious, are placed in glass display cabinets. Religious plaques, prayers and philosophical comments such as 'What is a Home without Mother' or 'Home is where the Heart is' are elaborately framed and hung alongside all manner of cheap prints and picture-postcard calendars on walls. Tobacco packets with romantic names such as 'Rum Maple', 'Swan', 'Boxer' lie on tables next to partially burnt cigarettes rolled from newspaper. Gardens of homes are usually dry, unkempt and overgrown with weeds, and often contain evidence of attempts at the cultivation of some sort of vegetables.

It is against this background that I encountered my subjects and interacted with them. Their stories and accounts of their lives enhanced my understanding of this reality and I recorded them.
Johan du Toit, a warm-hearted 23-year-old, lived in Groot Marico with his mother, brother and two sisters, one of whom had an illegitimate child, in a corrugated-iron house with exposed wooden rafters and no electricity. He told me

> I applied for work in this town as a hydraulic assistant. There was no work for me. I didn't have papers. Anyway, the papers don't do the work. I got a job over at the mine last week checking vehicles before they were allowed on site. They made me stand outside like sheep when it rained, and would not let me go home to sleep. One day I felt so tired I fell asleep by the gate. The mine manager, a big, fat man, started kicking and cursing me. He ordered me off the property, and said he would kill me if I came near the place again.

A few years later I came across a more confident Johan. He had become a trader, catering for the blacks in tribal areas.

> I fill my truck chock full of all sorts of stuff from cooking pans to packets of yeast and chilli powder. I know the right 'coolies' so I get what I need at rock-bottom prices. I have learnt where there are no shops in the native locations. The blacks have plenty of money, plenty of cash, hungry stomachs, and no shops.

Until recently whites who could not get jobs in the private sector were guaranteed work in state companies such as the South African Railways. It was not unusual to meet simple and uneducated people who had secured employment with the railways and who could describe exotic places in Botswana, Zaire, Zambia, Namibia and Malawi where they had travelled when they worked on the trains.

Mr Eric Stanely, who now lives in the Orange Free State near the Lesotho border, casually told me:

> I was a ticket puncher for the S.A.R. for thirty years. During that time I travelled all over Africa. I know the blacks better than they know themselves. I ate porridge with them and tended sheep with them when I was a child. That was before apartheid. Then my young wife died in the Congo, many years ago, of fever. There were no drugs or doctors available. I sat around helplessly staring and had to bury her when she was gone. Africa is depressing. The whites brought some civilization. They brought the trains, but were forced to leave. Now things are going downhill.

A railway worker, recently made redundant as a result of privatization:

> I hitched to Namibia, could not get work, I came back home in the back of a truck full of sheep. Then I went to Zimbabwe and got deported after, in a bar full of soldiers one night, I called the president a 'communist whore'. I should have known better. It's become dangerous now in South Africa. If I can't get a ride by the time it gets dark I sleep in police cells. They don't seem to mind in the small stations so long as I give the policemen a few beers and leave the next morning. Life was much easier working for the railways. At least we had a uniform, respect, and a roof over our head.

Some of the down and outers who have experienced failure, most particularly in farming which is drought-prone, are seized by the romantic notion of diamond digging. In the vicinity of old river beds, thought to be filled with millions of years of diamond-bearing gravels, I encountered this phenomenon. They leave behind all their possessions and live frugally in portable zinc-sheeted houses. It is common practice for an entire savings to be gambled on the chance of finding the ultimate stone. Suspicion, jealousy and thievery are prevalent, and 'claim jumping' is common. Rumours of 'big finds' and 'lost fortunes' abound, and sensational news spreads like wild fire. Euphoria, disappointment and disillusionment are the stuff of the lives of these weather-beaten people.

Year upon year of political instability, cultural boycotts and sanctions have created an inward looking isolationism that has pervaded all levels of South African society. In the extremely insular platteland, esoteric religious beliefs, tradition and folklore are intricately woven into the fabric of everyday life. The Bible is revered and often quoted. Valuables are kept in metal boxes, and buried in secret places in the ground. Beds are elevated on cement-filled paint tins or on old bricks to keep evil spirits away at night. So as to be prepared to shoot an intruder, a common practice is to sleep fully clothed with a pistol close by. People sometimes store planks for prospective coffins.

Generally, sex is considered taboo, not to be discussed. Charlene van der Westhuizen, a divorcee who spends most of her time either looking after her retarded son or working in the local candle factory, confided:

> I got married when I was nineteen. My father was very strict, and I grew up on a farm far away from anything. Before I got married I had never been to a cinema or even a dance. Not until I had my first baby did I realise what it was all about. I thought children were born by a man putting his private parts on a woman's navel.

The repressive nature of the apartheid system pervades all sexual matters. The Immorality Act prohibited sexual relations between members of different races and the system of censorship banned all material perceived to be sexually provocative. However, an overt preoccupation with sexuality is conspicuous in the display of nudes on the pages of local publications that I saw unselfconsciously and immodestly hung on the walls of living rooms of many platteland homes. In fact, I noticed growing prostitution and increased promiscuity. There were casual relationships between whites and blacks in the very midst of mainstream 'conservatism'.

Mr Le Roux, a pensioner who once worked for the Department of Mines and now has trouble walking as a result of being hit by a bulldozer, was outspoken about his activities:

> The 'kaffir girls' in the platteland are cheap. All they want is beer and meat and a bed to sleep in. White women just give you problems. A black woman costs you five smackeroos a week, a white one, over three hundred.
> The people here hate my guts. My neighbours saved up and bought my last house I was renting. I then bought another place around the corner and brought my girl-friends with me. The same monkeys are trying to get rid of me again, but now that the Group Areas Act is gone they can stew.

Mr Le Roux rambled on about starting a 'striptease joint' near the goldfields in the Orange Free State, but recognized that he did not have the kind of courage it would take. He thought he might be 'tarred and feathered like the niggers in America'.

A middle-aged, gaunt Mrs van der Westhuizen who had spent long periods of time alone due to her husband's job as a locomotive driver for the railways, told me:

> I don't like it here. People talk about each other all the time. They spread lies and rumours. The townspeople accuse me of sleeping with black men and hoboes, of being a witch. The neighbours' children are often throwing dead black cats on my front lawn. People here just have nothing better to think about.

Yet a strong sense of kinship is apparent in communities that I encountered, and it was often difficult to distinguish between family members and mere associates. In more disadvantaged circumstances interbreeding often occurred due to naivety and the fact that limited living space resulted in close physical proximity between family members. As a result, incidences of congenital disease, deformity and retardation occur within particular communities. In the more remote areas of the country, especially in the Karoo, interbreeding has occurred over decades and even centuries.

In many families, feuds and squabbles persist and gossip, rumours and intrigue occupy much time. Recollections and discussions of misfortune predominate.

A small fine-boned woman from the Groot Marico district, whom I have come to know well over time, recounted how the first husband she had married, a close friend of hers, had absconded with all their possessions a few months after their wedding; her second husband, a brother of this fugitive, had died of a heart attack the day of their wedding, and how she had recently lost a third husband to suicide a week after marriage.

Another woman, Mrs Davis of the Western Cape, at first bashful about being seen with curlers in her hair, described to me how, returning from her father's funeral, she had found her childhood home bulldozed to the ground by her son, a machine operator in a construction company. Her son had been ashamed of the home in which his mother and grandfather shared a bedroom. Having nowhere else to go, she had moved into what had once been the 'servants' quarters' which was the only edifice left standing on the property. Then her son managed to escape from the local jail where he was being held as a result of the first deed and, finding her alone, tied her up and began systematically to dismantle what was left. He even went as far as to saw down a centuries-old poplar which, at one time, had provided shade from the hot Kalahari sun. The newly felled timber and dehydrated leaves were left on what had once been the front lawn.

As a result of the scarcity of doctors and prescription drugs in the past, numerous home remedies have evolved for common ailments, for heart and circulatory problems, including high blood pressure, digestive disorders, conditions of the respiratory system and depression and anxiety. Herbs and home-grown vegetables are mixed with various concoctions of animal blood, urine and crushed ants. In some parts of the country, particularly in the Western Transvaal, mampoer, or whisky made from a wild fruit relished by elephants, is a cure-all. Some medicinal preparations (readily available in cafés and concession stores) such as Vaseline, Vicks and Grandpa headache powder, an Aspirin derivative, are used as remedies for almost all conditions. For toothache, brushing one's teeth with petrol has been found to relieve the pain. If all else fails traditional witchdoctors are consulted to 'suss out' evil and counteract bad influences.

Mrs L Oosthuizen who has become bedridden, stated:

> I hear voices from close by and far away. The rats in my roof drive me mad at night. Last night I felt so sick that I went to see a witchdoctor. He gave me muti, a green powder to mix with milk. It made me so sick that I thought I was going to die. I feel like I am going to go mad, mad in my body and in my heart. My son, Hank, and I argued not long ago. He left angrily and wasn't seen for weeks. He was found by Bushmen at the bottom of an old mineshaft, dead.
> My neck does not stop jerking, whatever the time of day it is; it's uncontrollable. I'm sure the coloured man is back by the willow tree hitting frogs. I must go and see a witchdoctor today to break the spell.

A woman who had been told she could not have children eventually bore two in close succession. She called them Charles and Diana, after the British monarchy, because she said they were so precious that they were her prince and princess. She told me that she had been so scared that the children would fall prey to a witchdoctor that she had moved away from the platteland to Johannesburg. Her ex-neighbour's baby had disappeared one day, and was found headless and limbless in the caves near the farm she lived on.

Psychiatric help is almost unheard of in platteland communities. In most regions, there are a few so-called social workers who visit individuals unable to help themselves. They are usually concerned with seeing to it that 'unbalanced' people have basic foodstuffs, that their government compensation cheques have been received and cashed, and that they are not a danger to the community.

Selma, a single mother living in a rundown shack next to the Orange River, was partly ignored, partly pitied by her neighbours. A local shopkeeper spoke about her:

> Selma? She's mad. Her house looks like a bomb hit it. There are spider webs and dust everywhere you look. She collects old junk from the diamond diggers and stores it all over her house and in her garage. The fence around her house is made from the bumpers of cars. Bones from her meals are buried all over her lawn. She has twelve cats in her house that never go outside. Even the social workers avoid her. Once she starts talking nothing can stop her. She is like a machine gun shooting off. When she gets irritated she climbs on top of her corrugated iron roof and bangs on it. Sometimes she lifts up her skirt to all who walk by.

Children with problems are usually sent by social workers to special schools in the larger towns. Most parents blame their children's disabilities on fevers, knocks on their heads during childhood, or on ill-defined diseases labelled meningitis, encephalitis or tickbite fever. Meisie, the wife of a woodcutter located near Knysna, commented about her daughter:

Tani got encephalitis from bad water when she was five. Next year she will go to school far away from here. My Tani is a slow learner, but once she learns something she never forgets. She knows everyone's birthdays - all the aunts and uncles, cousins, sisters and brothers. She's special. She can put her body in all sorts of inside-out positions. The circus wanted her, but my girl's too young and the pay is bad, and she would always be travelling.

In the past few years, Satanism as a form of worship has become more than just a peripheral movement as traditional values centering around church and family erode. Whilst one reads of occasional incidents of human sacrifice, most bloodletting is confined to rituals involving chickens, goats, and sometimes dogs. I have seen people smear themselves with animal fat or blood, put mice in their pockets and, dressed in black, go to graveyards and dance around tombstones. Oaths, signed in blood, pledge loyalty to the cult. On one particular occasion, I happened on a house of a satanic leader in a small semi-deserted town in the northern Cape near Namibia. The main bedroom contained a complex music system with numerous speakers painted dark pink. Nailed onto the walls were dolls of different hair colours. Needles were inserted into various parts of their bodies. In the middle of this same bedroom was a cracked toilet.

A young woman whose nails were almost as long as her fingers and painted black, and who claimed to be the daughter of a satanic priest, spoke vividly of her memories.

From the time I was small, I remember being carried from my bedside in the middle of the night. I always felt cold and scared. My father, a satanic priest, wore long shiny purple robes. After driving on dirty roads, we usually ended up at a big barn where a large fire was burning inside. Many of the people were dressed as gladiators, with leather leg straps, long knives attached to their belts, and funny hats sometimes with horns on them... Soon, there was blood all over. The sacrificed animals were put on a candle-lit table, and everybody would take turns stabbing the helpless beasts. Then after some time the group,

> chanting, would take the mutilated carcasses to shallow earthen pits. By the end of the night, whichever animals were not yet dead were tossed into one of these pits and then buried alive.

Crime and violence are increasing in the countryside. Many pensioners literally bar themselves into their homes, and farmers have banded together to form makeshift armies. The ownership of automatic weapons has proliferated. Farmers such as Mr R van der Vyfer, living in an isolated area near the Transkei, feel particularly vulnerable.

> Last month a 'burglar' broke through the kitchen window and stole our radio. I tried to shoot him, but I missed. There are no other whites living around here. We called the police, but they never came. I think they are scared themselves. They, too, fear for their lives. My 'boss boy' informed me that radical blacks from the Transkei are trying to force us off the land. They say it is their ancestors' land. I say it is mine 'cause I was born here. I say it was theirs fifty thousand years ago when there were no Europeans in Africa. I have nowhere else to go. To get me out of here they will have to get at me and my wife.

Until recently the platteland mentality assumed that supremacy was the natural providence of whites. They were protected by a legislature that granted them power, freedom and exclusive franchise as a birthright of being white. The political and social transformation that is occurring here brings with it spates of uncertainty, fear, anger and insecurity.

While militant whites have become vocal in their sinister aim to resist majority rule, I found that generally there was acknowledgement that change is inevitable. Mr P Streicher, an old man who remembered the Boer War at the turn of the century, commented:

> We are now at the crossroads. It's obvious. For us whites it looks like the end of an era. It is too late to stop change. The whites were on top for a long time. South Africa is part of Africa. It is a mistake to expect it to end differently.

The 'poor whites' had always relied upon the protective paternalism of the apartheid regime which enabled them to get by somehow. But the regime is dead, leaving behind a legacy of economic recession, isolation, repression, ignorance, social bigotry, political and racial disarray. So, too, has the mantle of assumed glory of white superiority fallen from their shoulders. They may well become another fragment of human detritus of the new South Africa.

Johan and Bertie, brothers, Western Transvaal, 1987

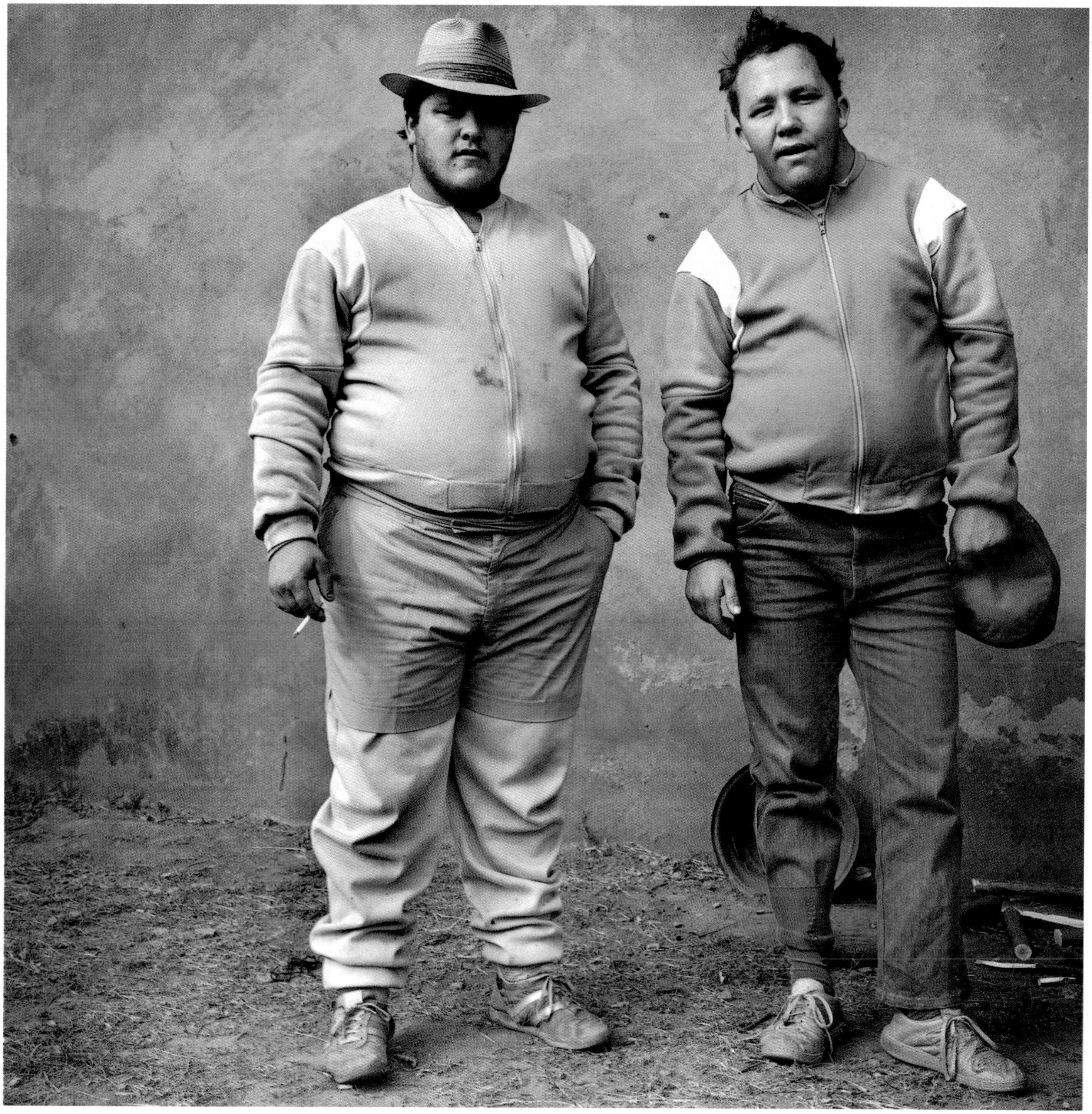

Annie Marie with daughter, Collie,
Western Transvaal, 1986

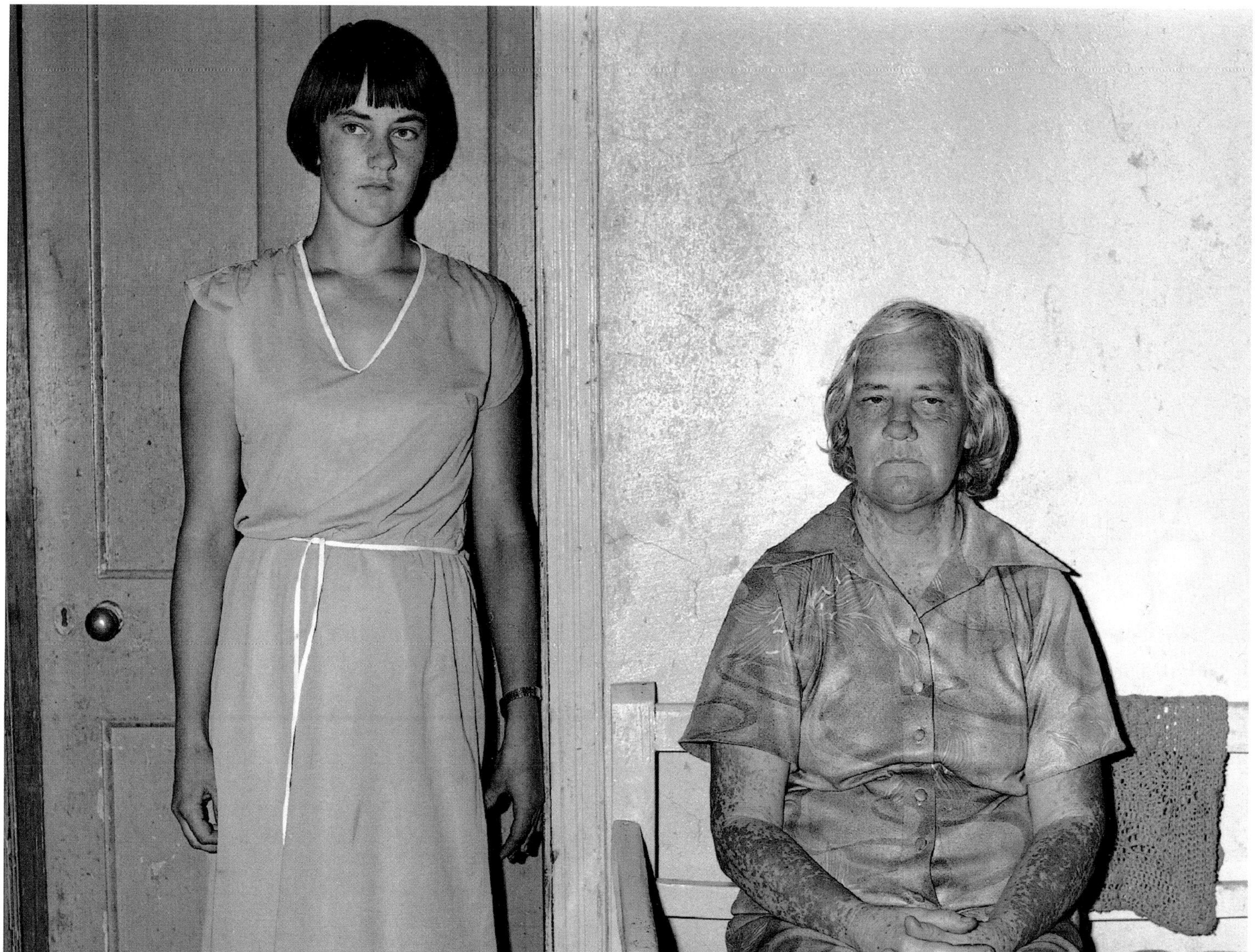

At du Toit, mine winder, Orange Free State, 1991

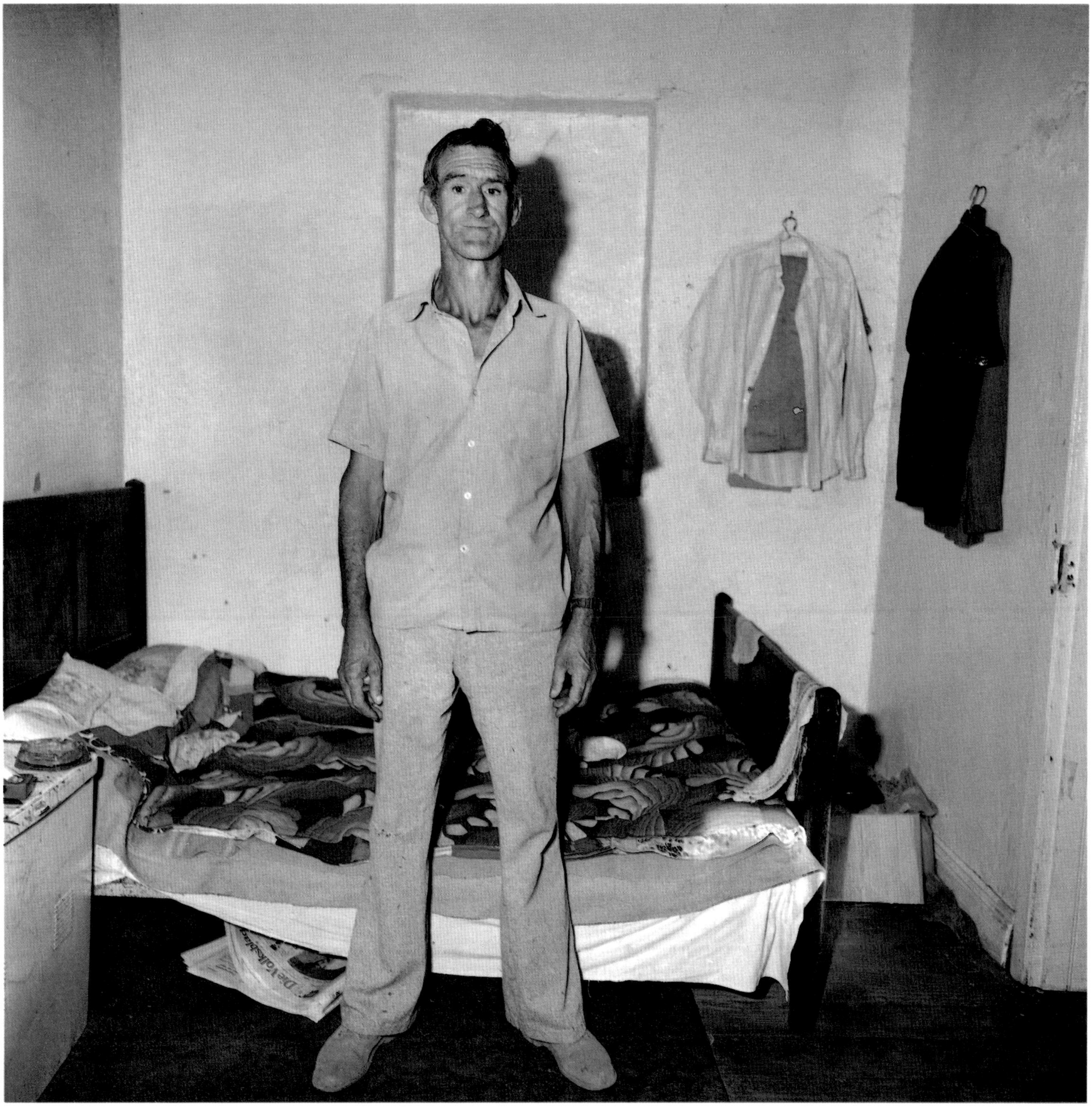

Divorcé, Southern Cape, 1990

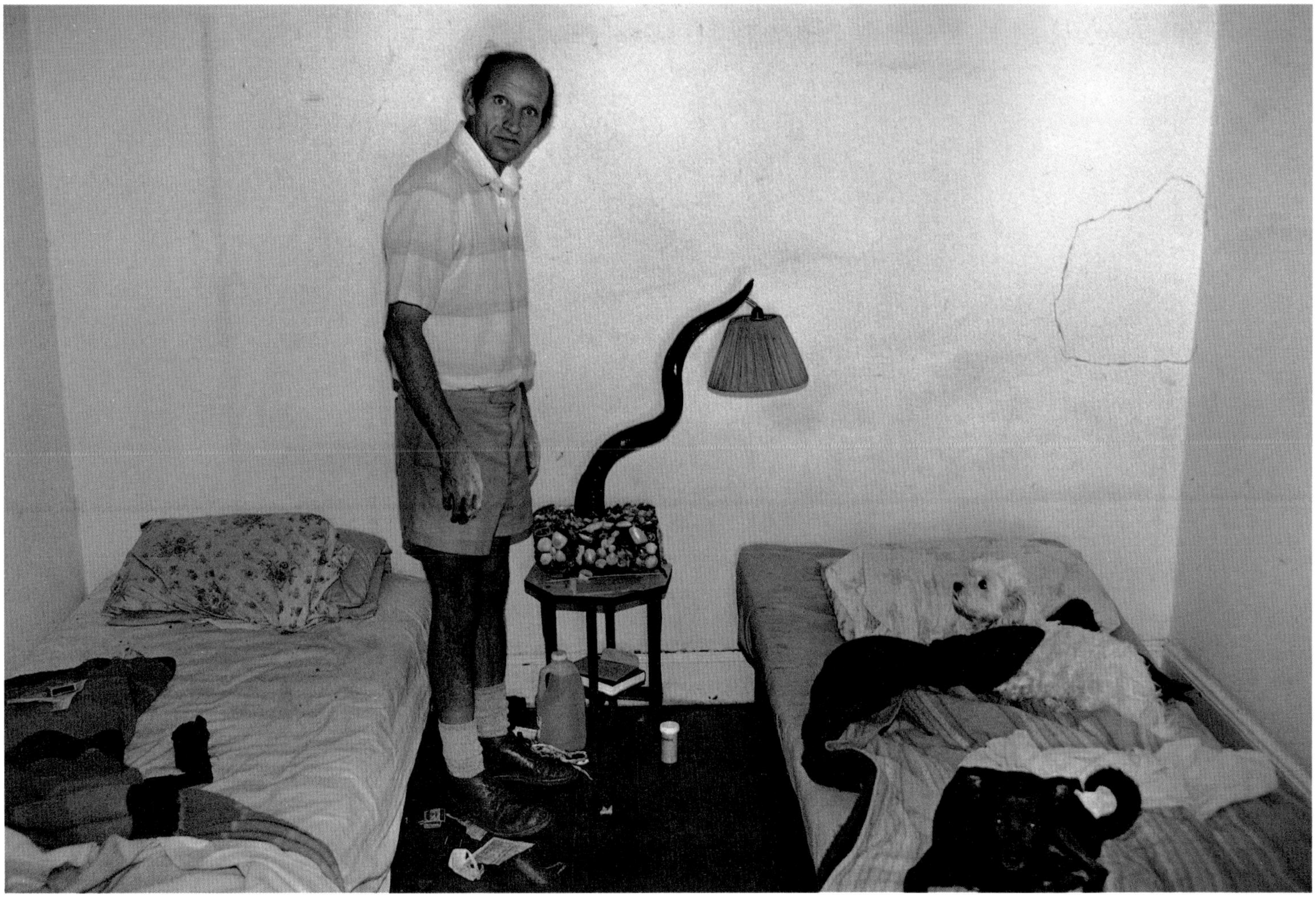

Man sleeping in children's room, Southern Cape, 1990

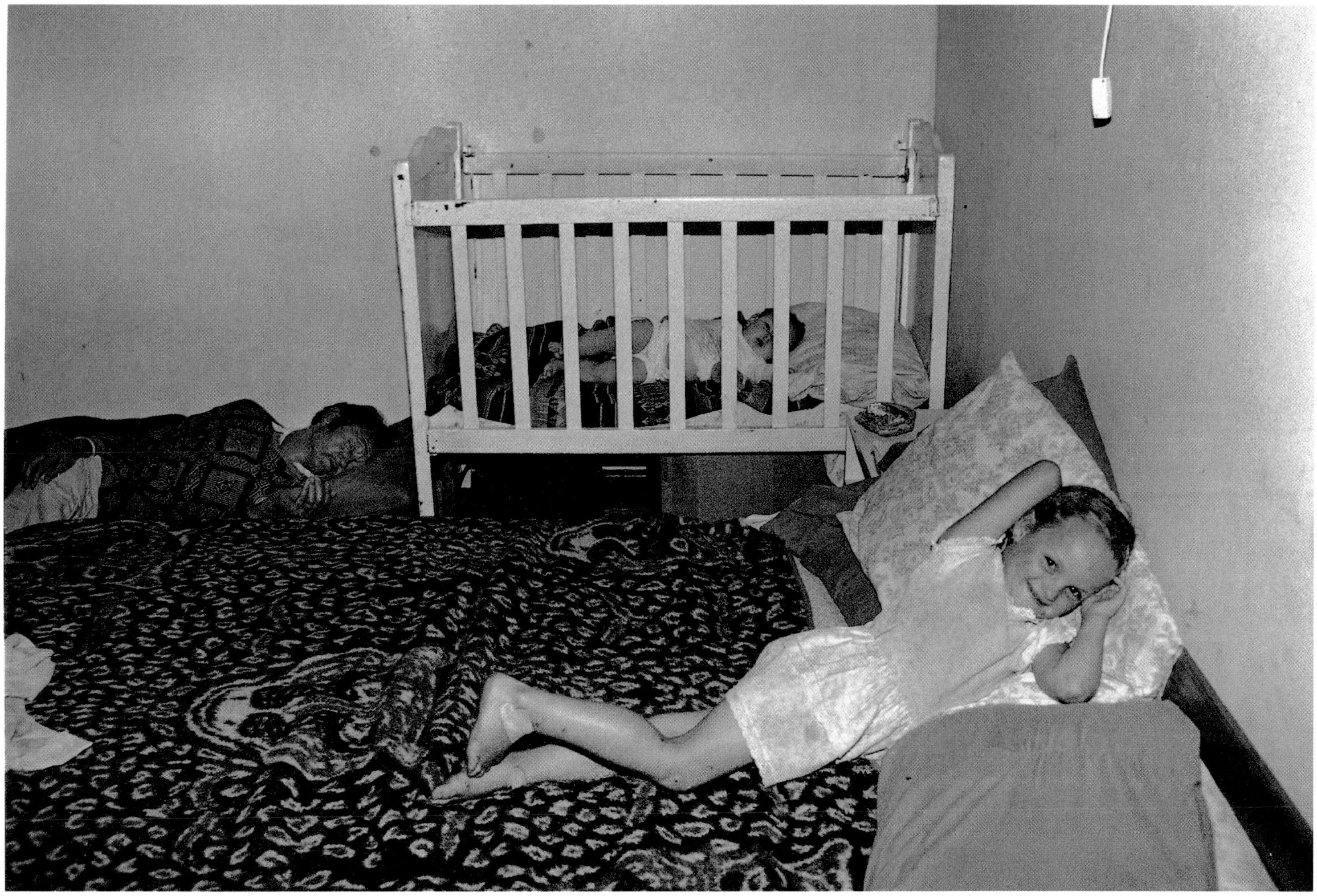

Boy with gun, girl with doll, mother with child,
Western Transvaal, 1992

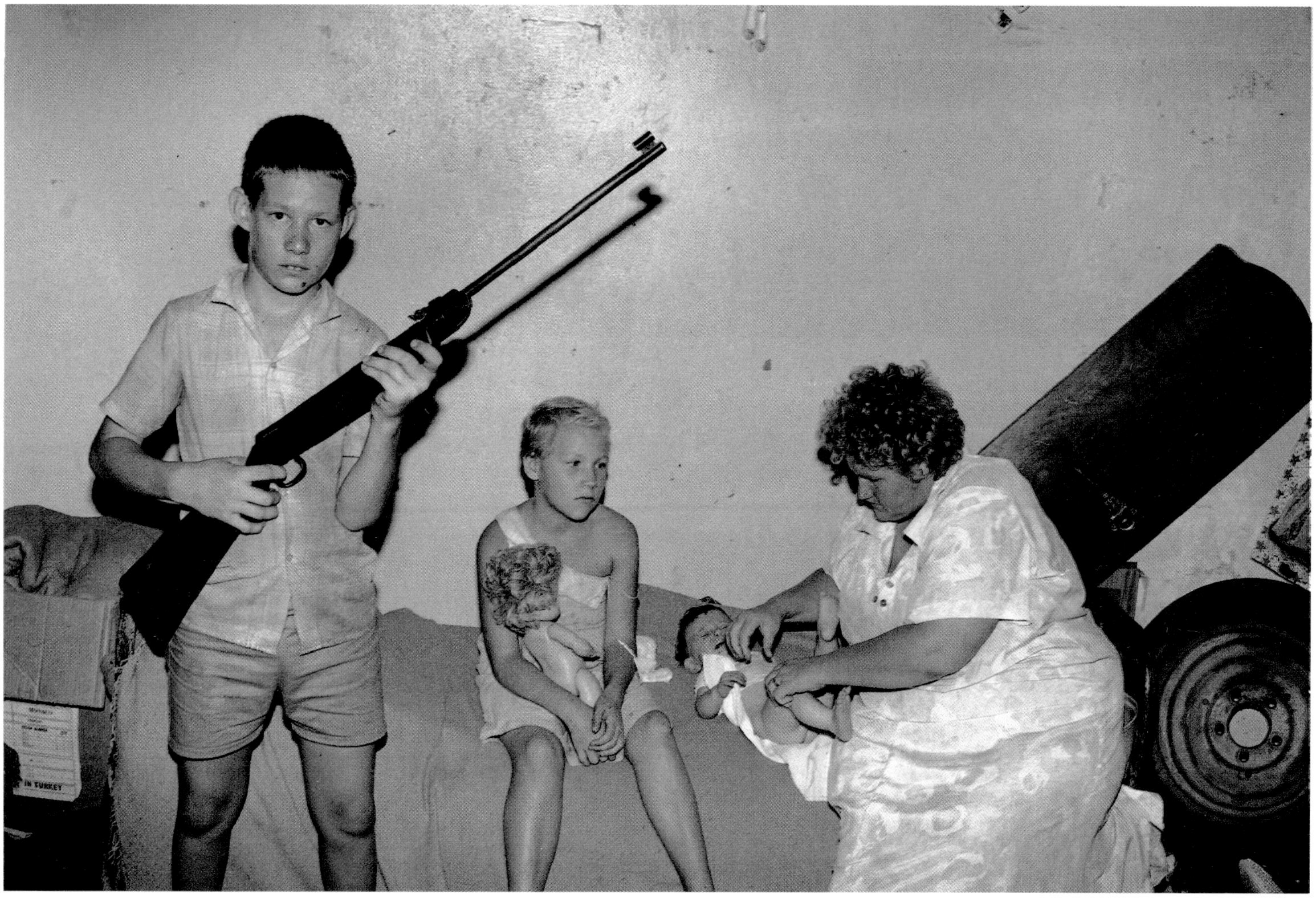
IN TURKEY

Sarie Fouche, candle factory employee, Orange Free State, 1992

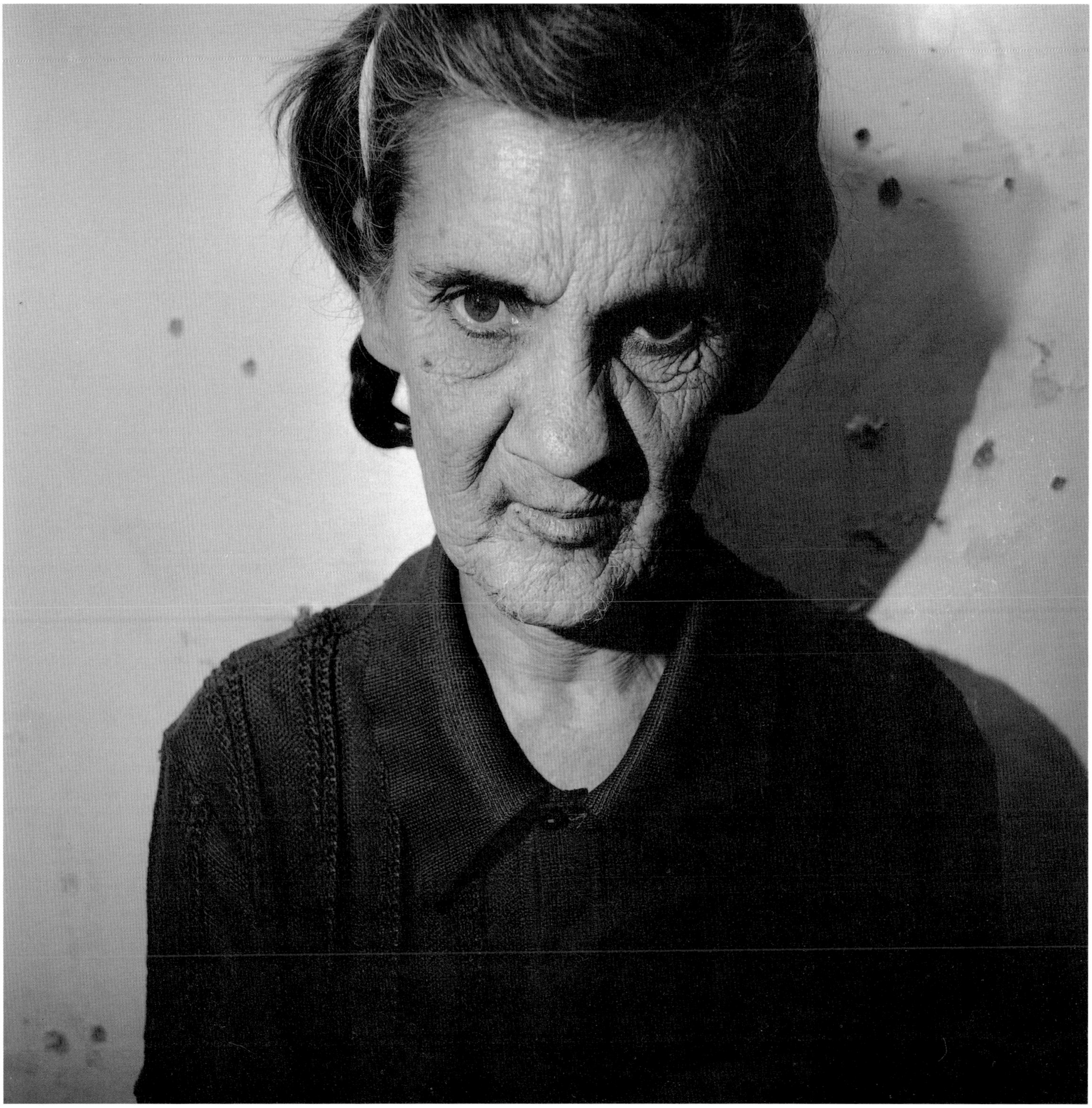

Prison warder and wife, Southern Transvaal, 1986

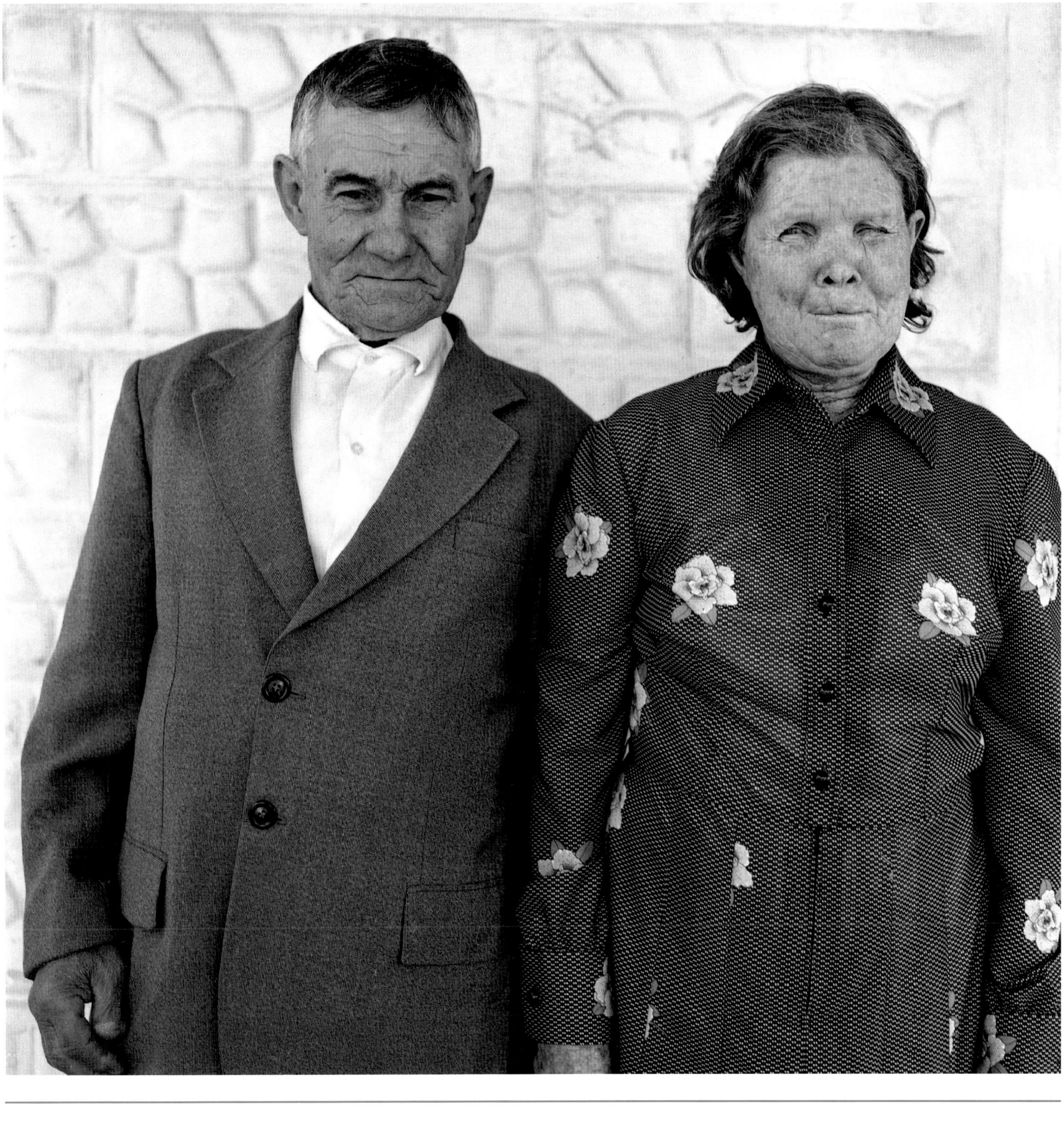

Woman and dogs, Orange Free State, 1994

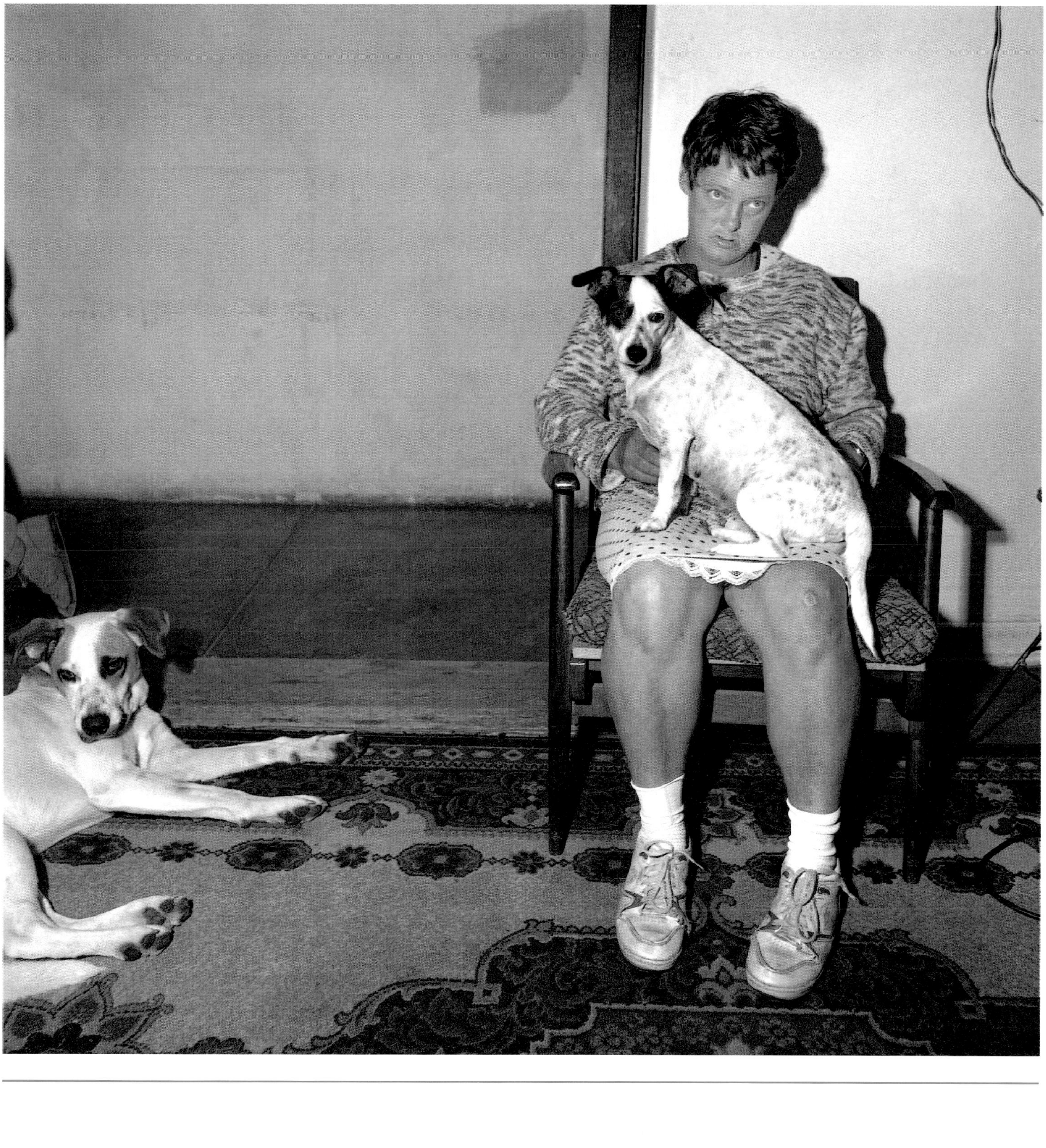

Dresie and Casie, twins, Western Transvaal, 1993

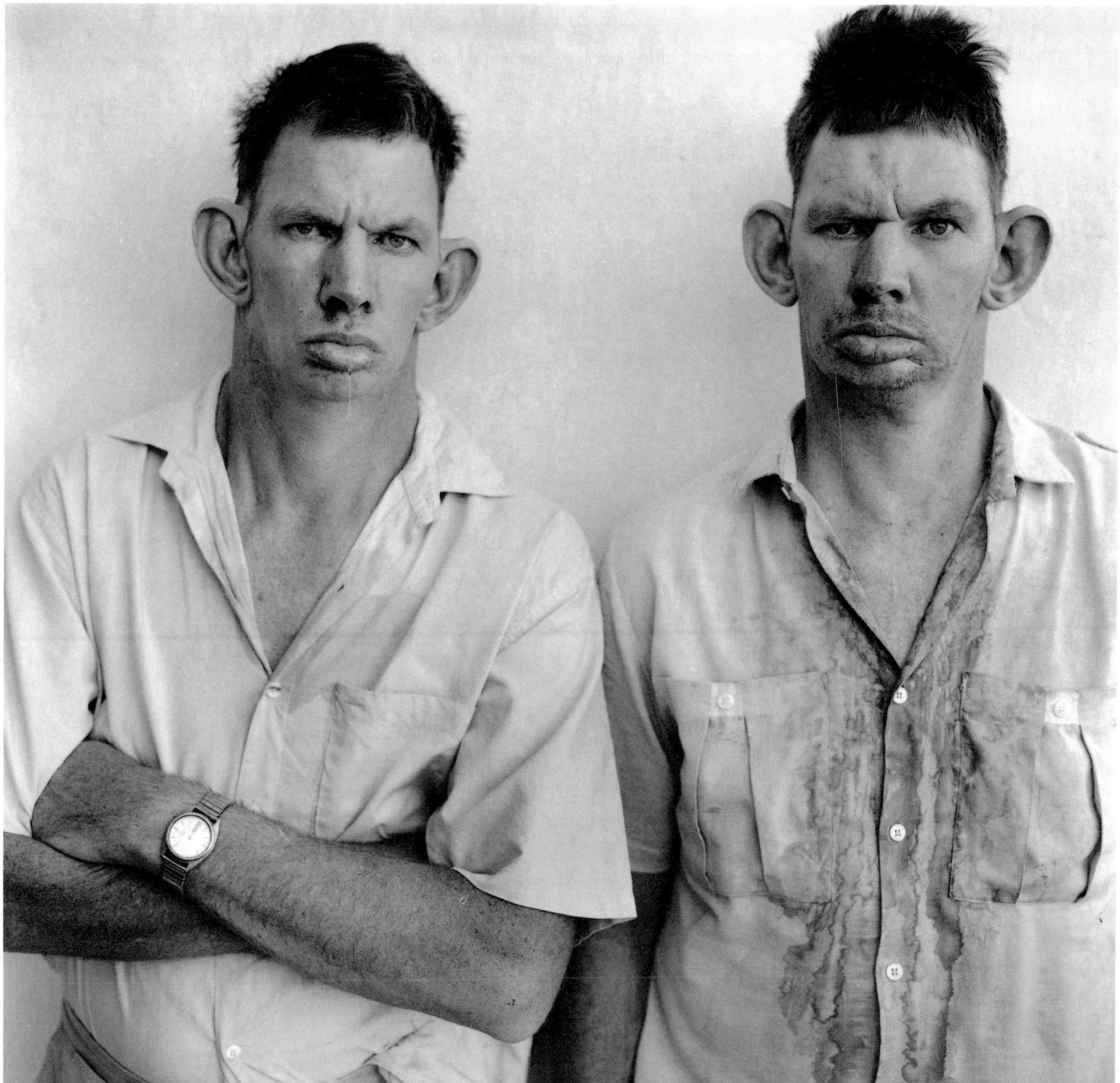

Mrs P R Streicher, Eastern Transvaal, 1993

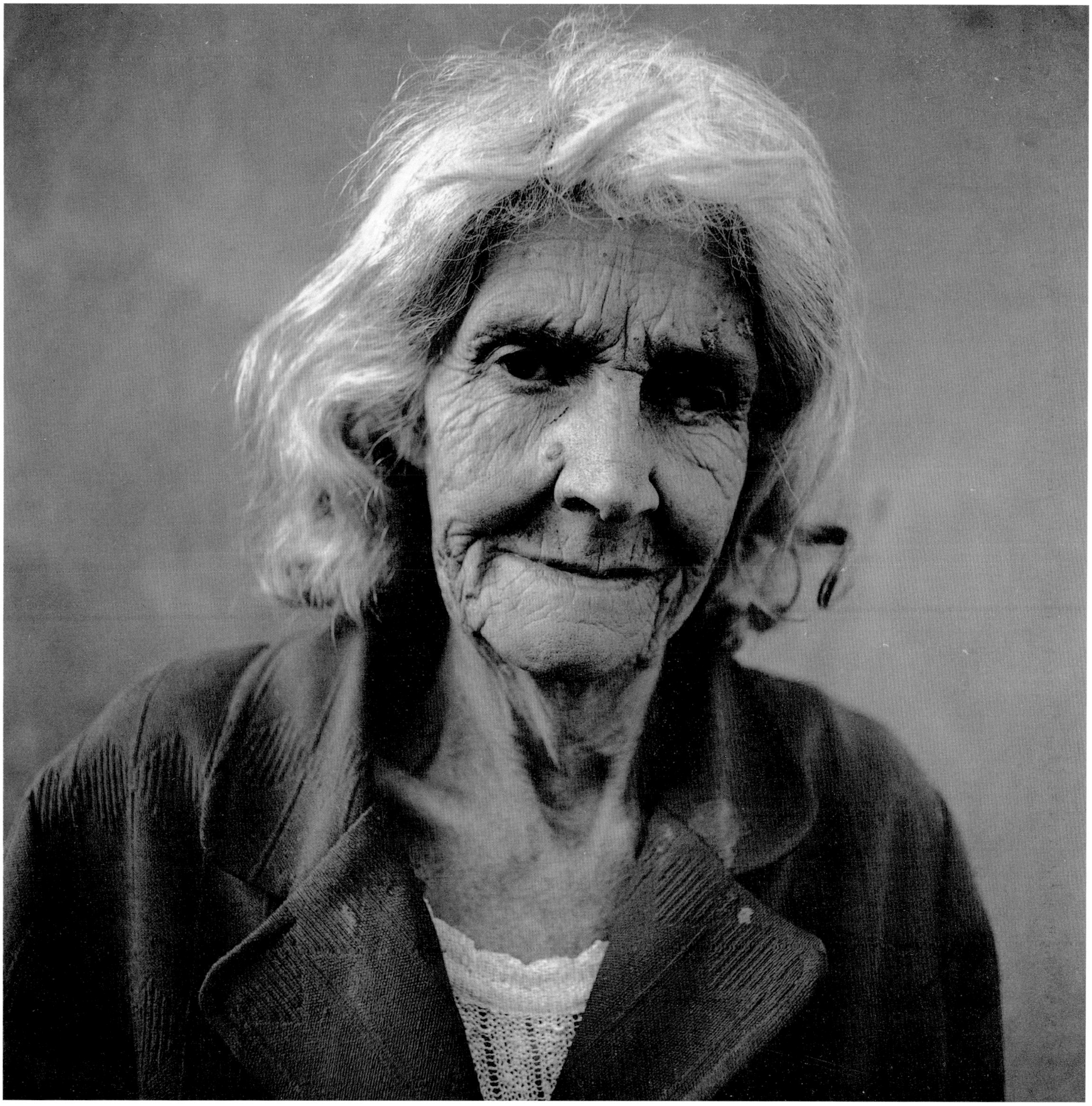

Deep-level gold miner in bedroom, Western Transvaal, 1987

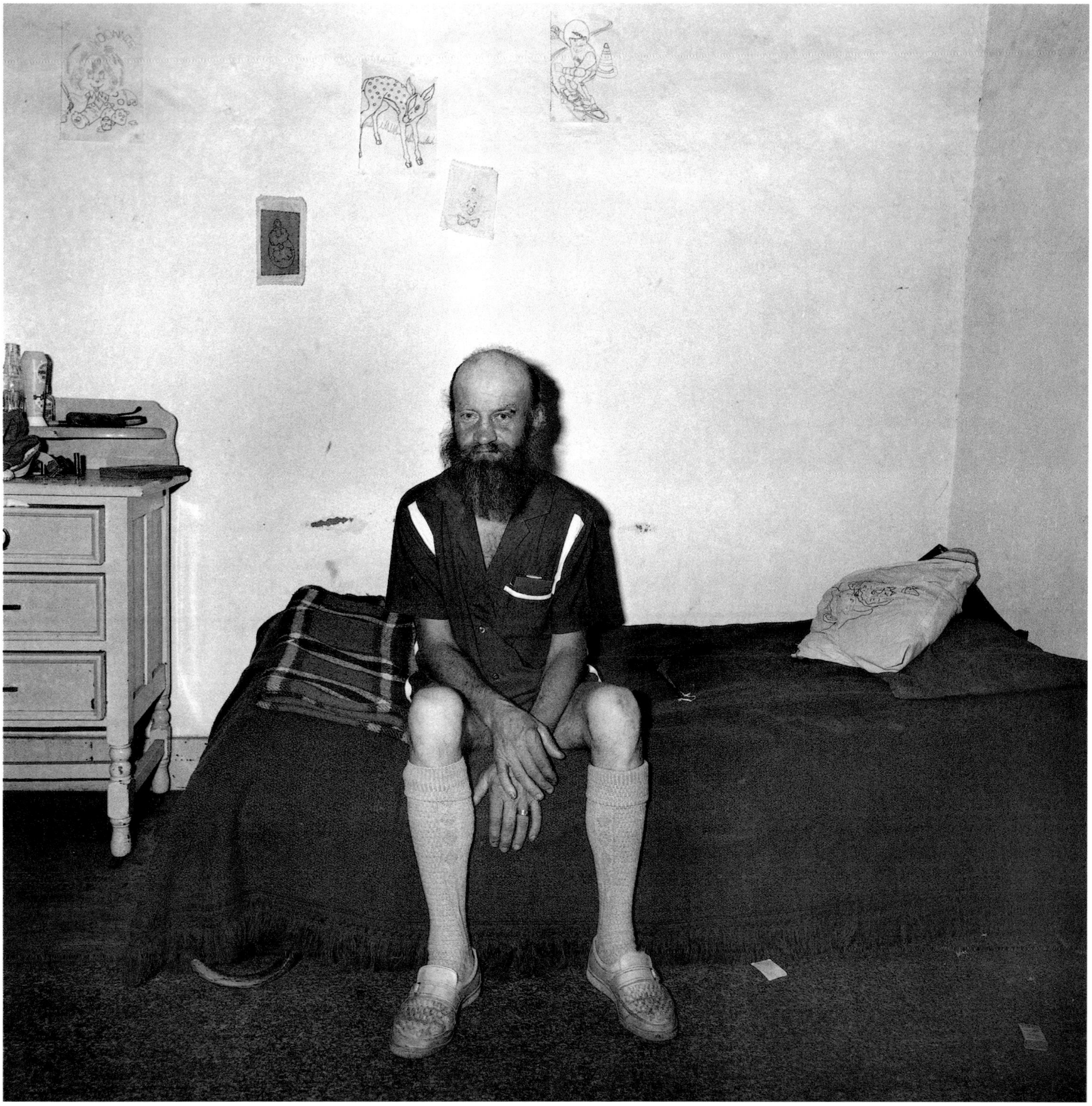

Man shaving on verandah, Western Transvaal, 1986

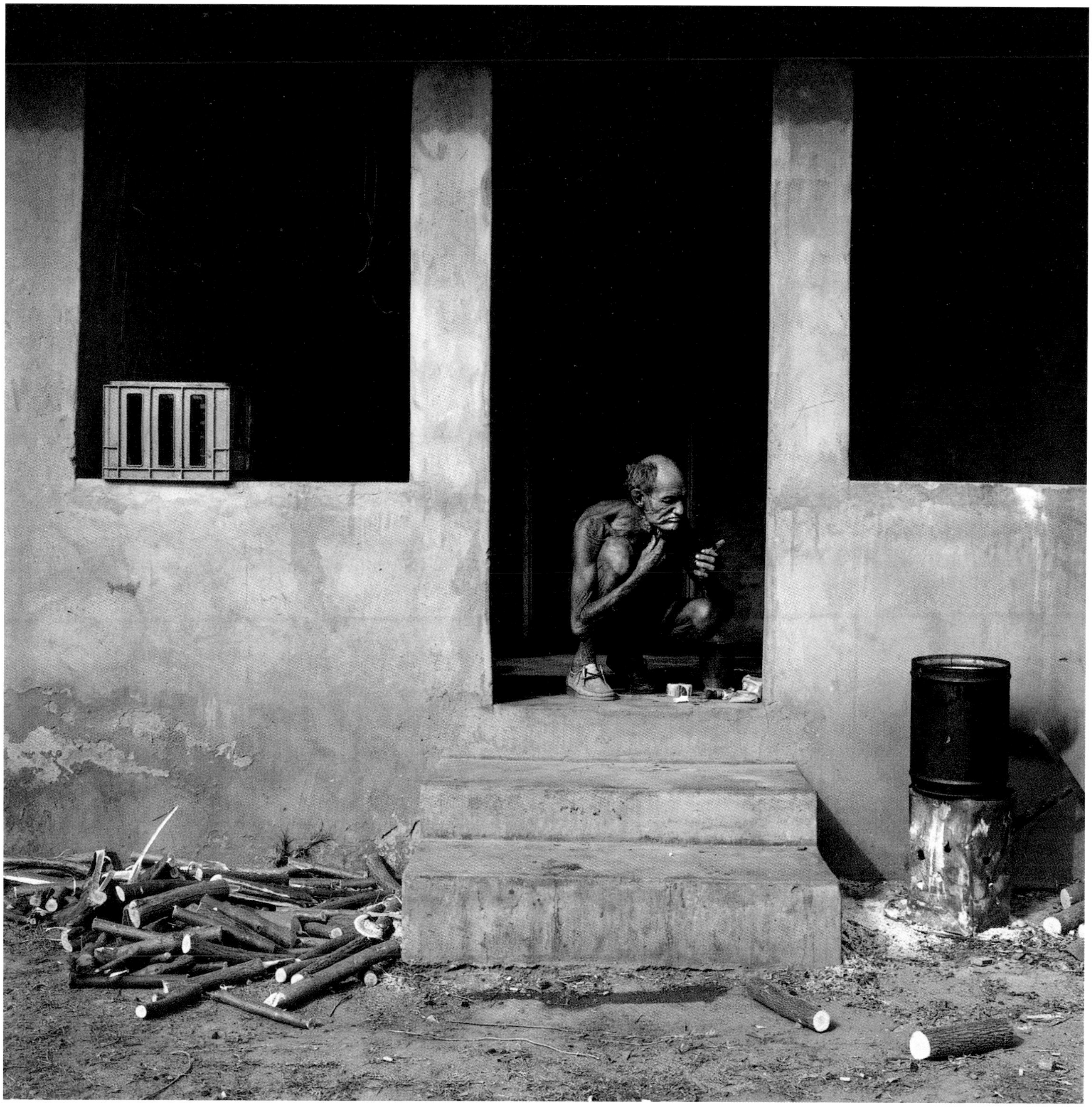

Prospectors inside house, Western Transvaal, 1987

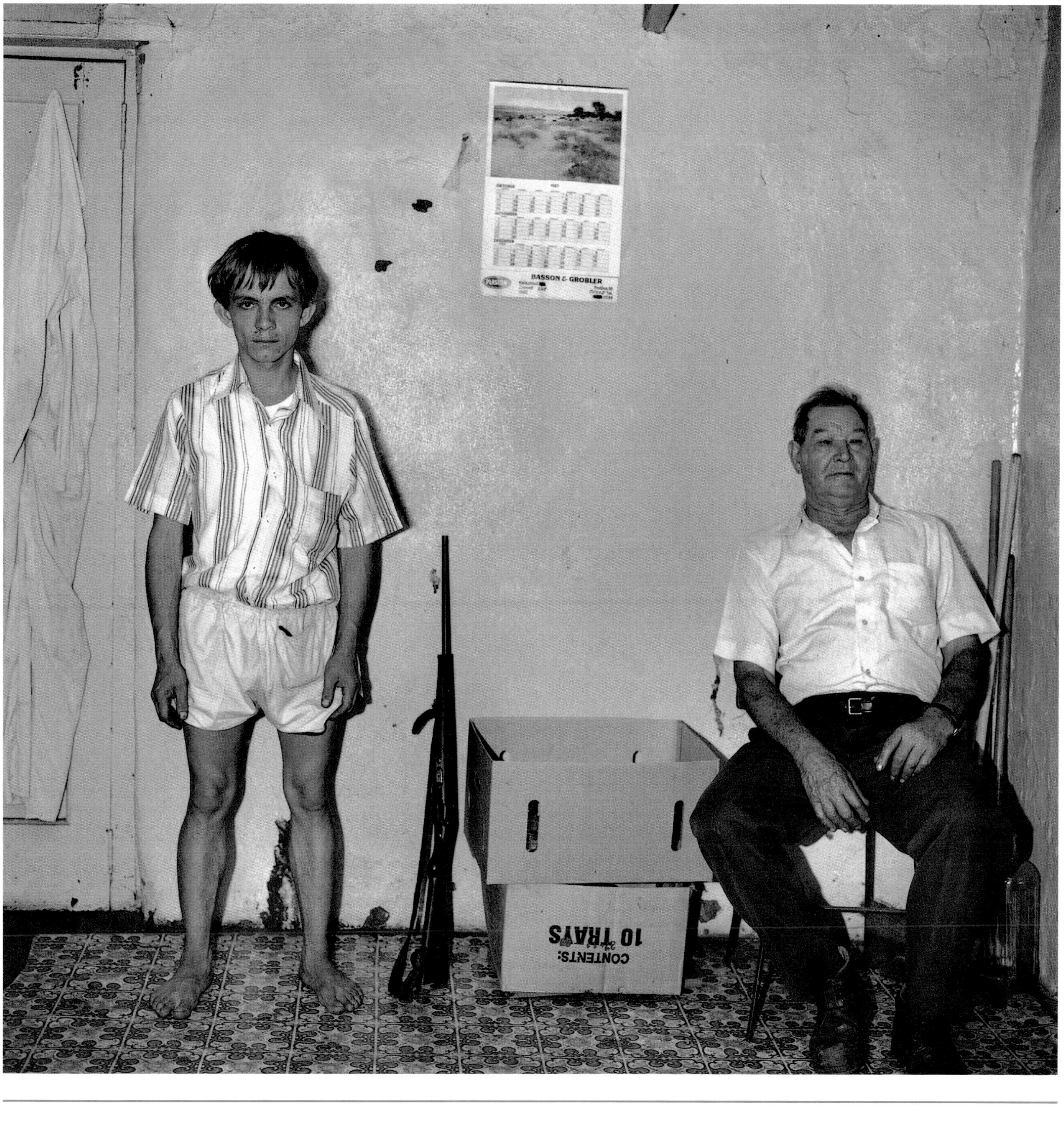
BASSON & GROBLER
CONTENTS:
10 TRAYS

Sergeant F de Bruin, Department of Prisons employee,
Orange Free State, 1992

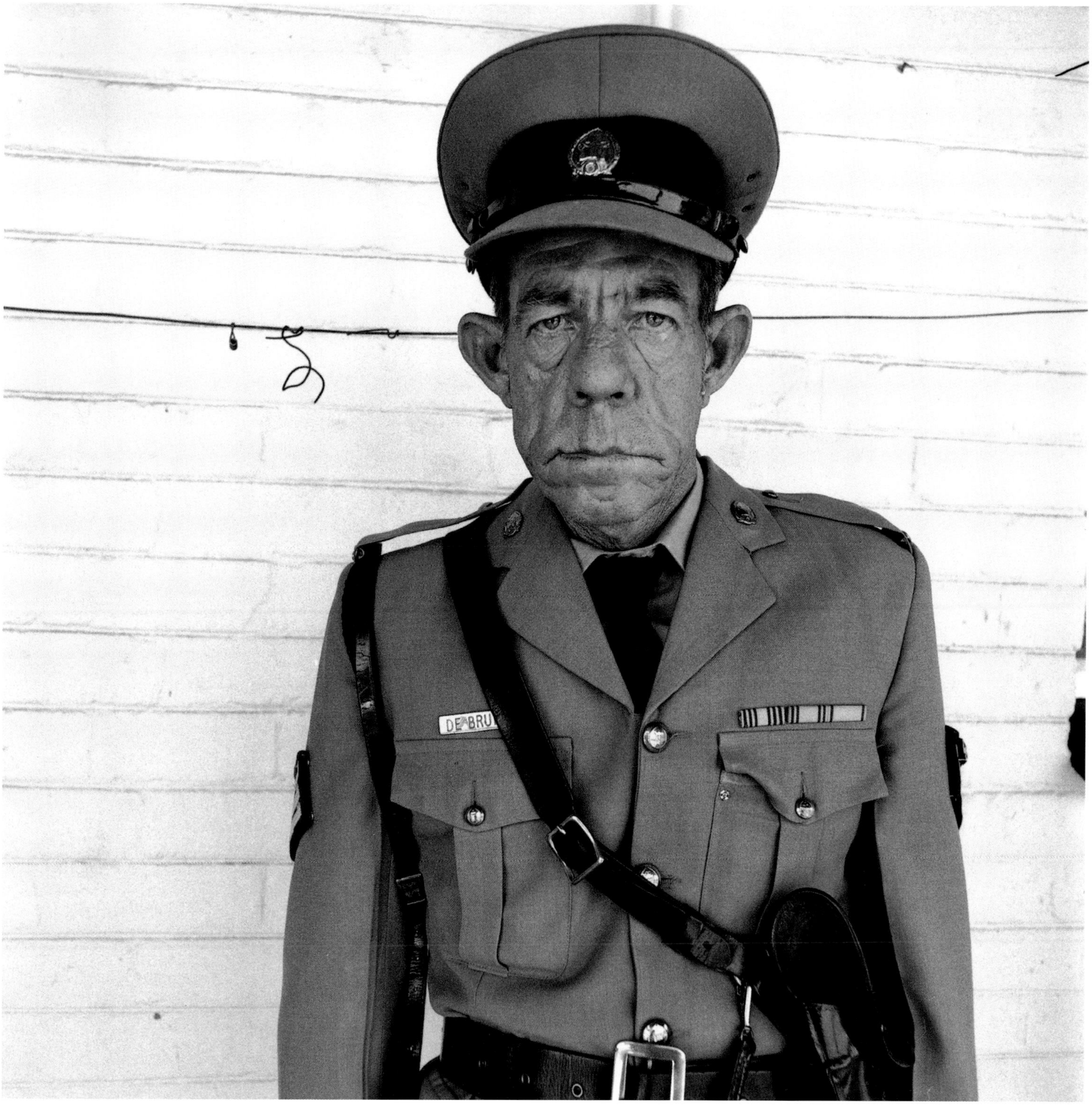

A Swart, goat farmer, Northern Cape, 1992

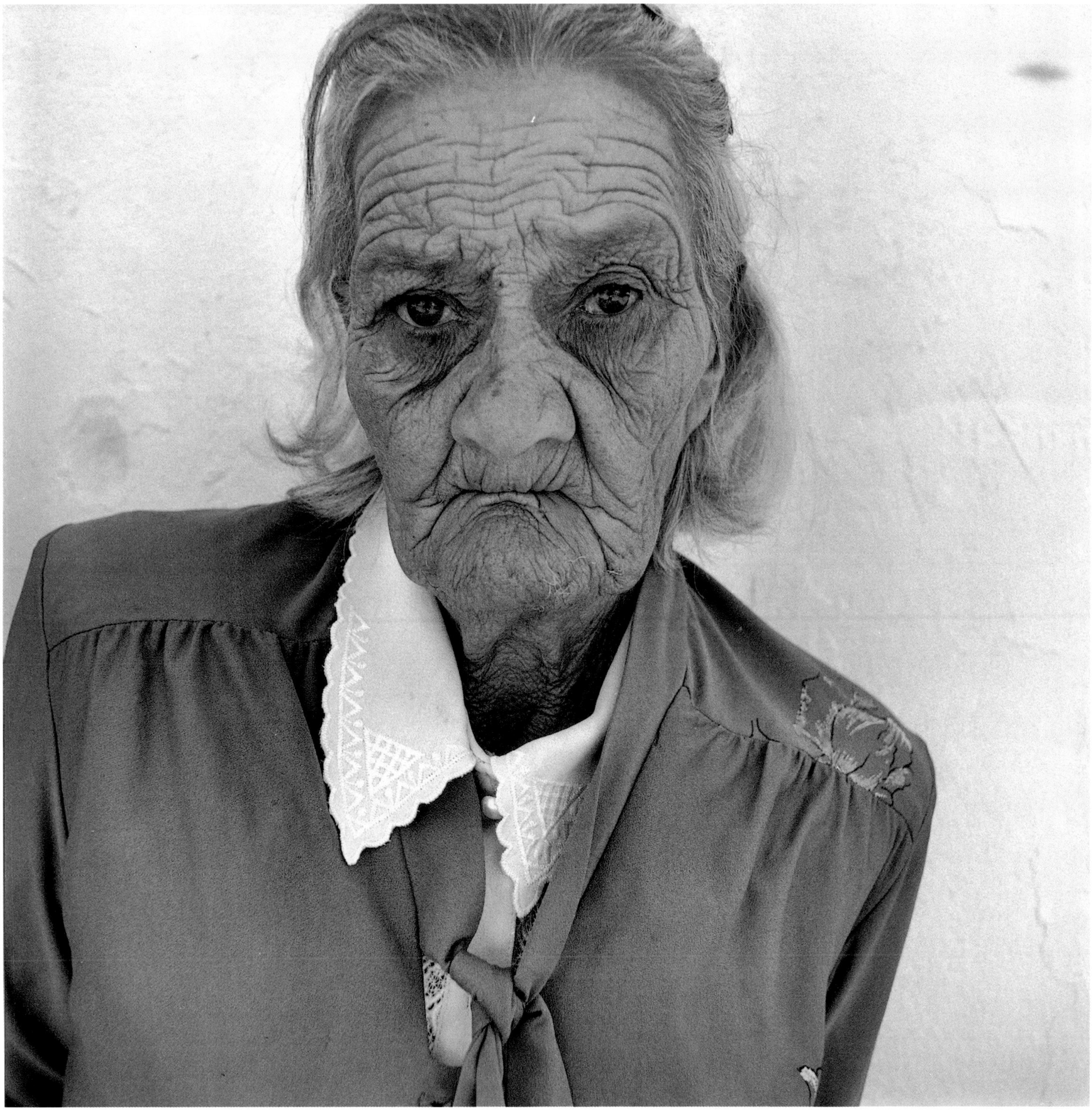

Henk Oosthuizen with sick mother,
Western Transvaal, 1988

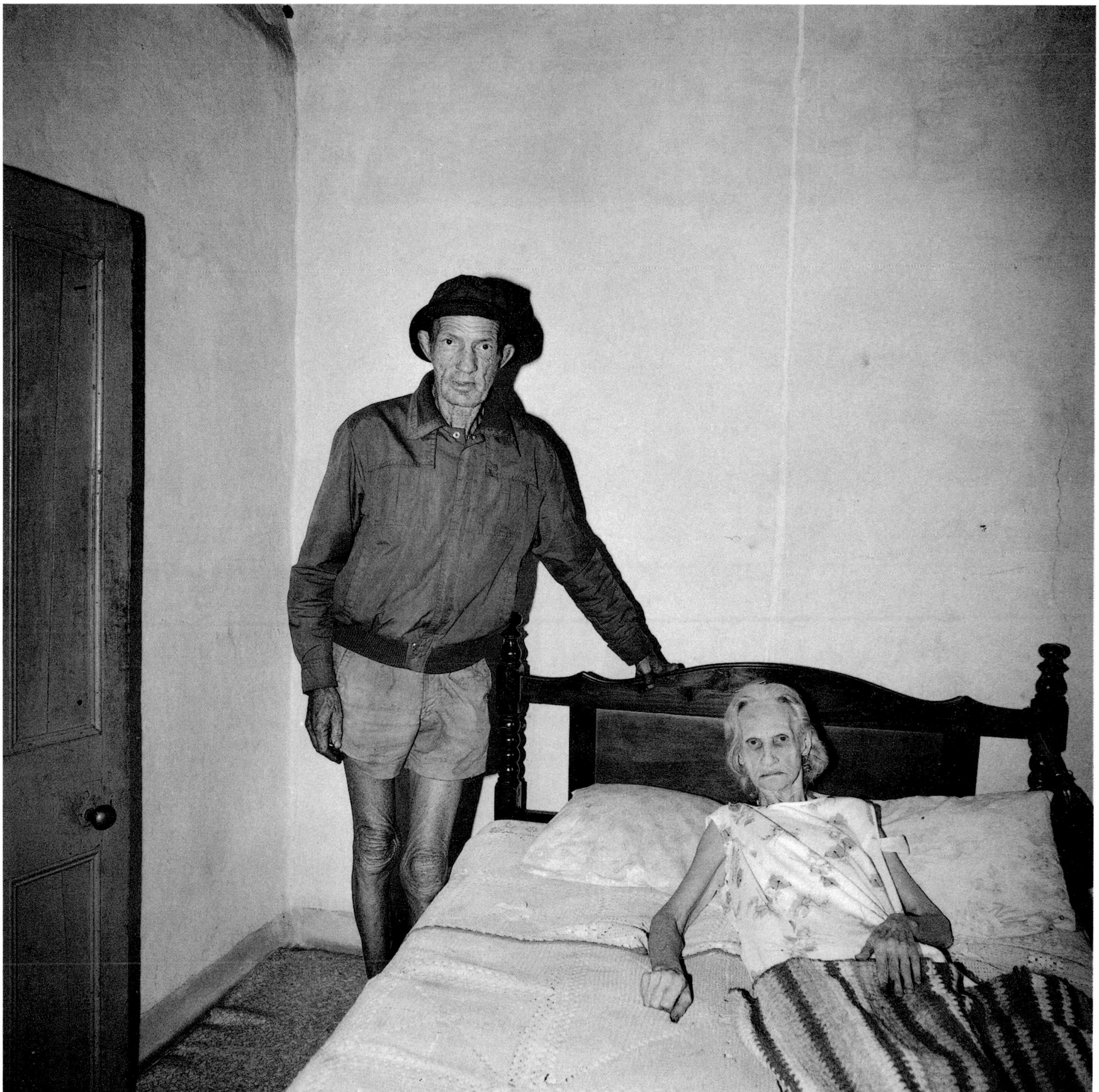

Gardener, Western Transvaal, 1993

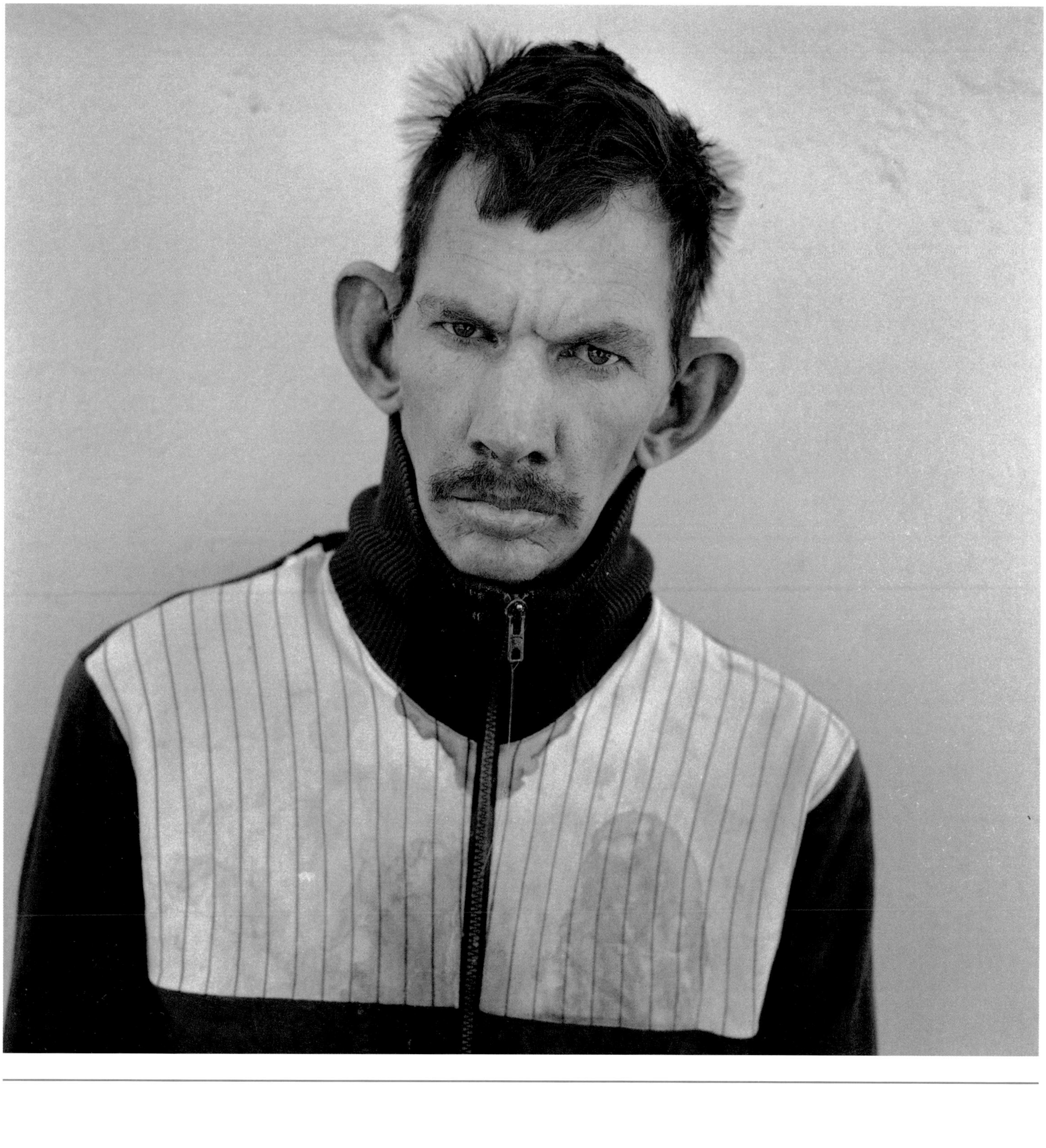

Municipal worker with pregnant wife, Western Transvaal, 1994

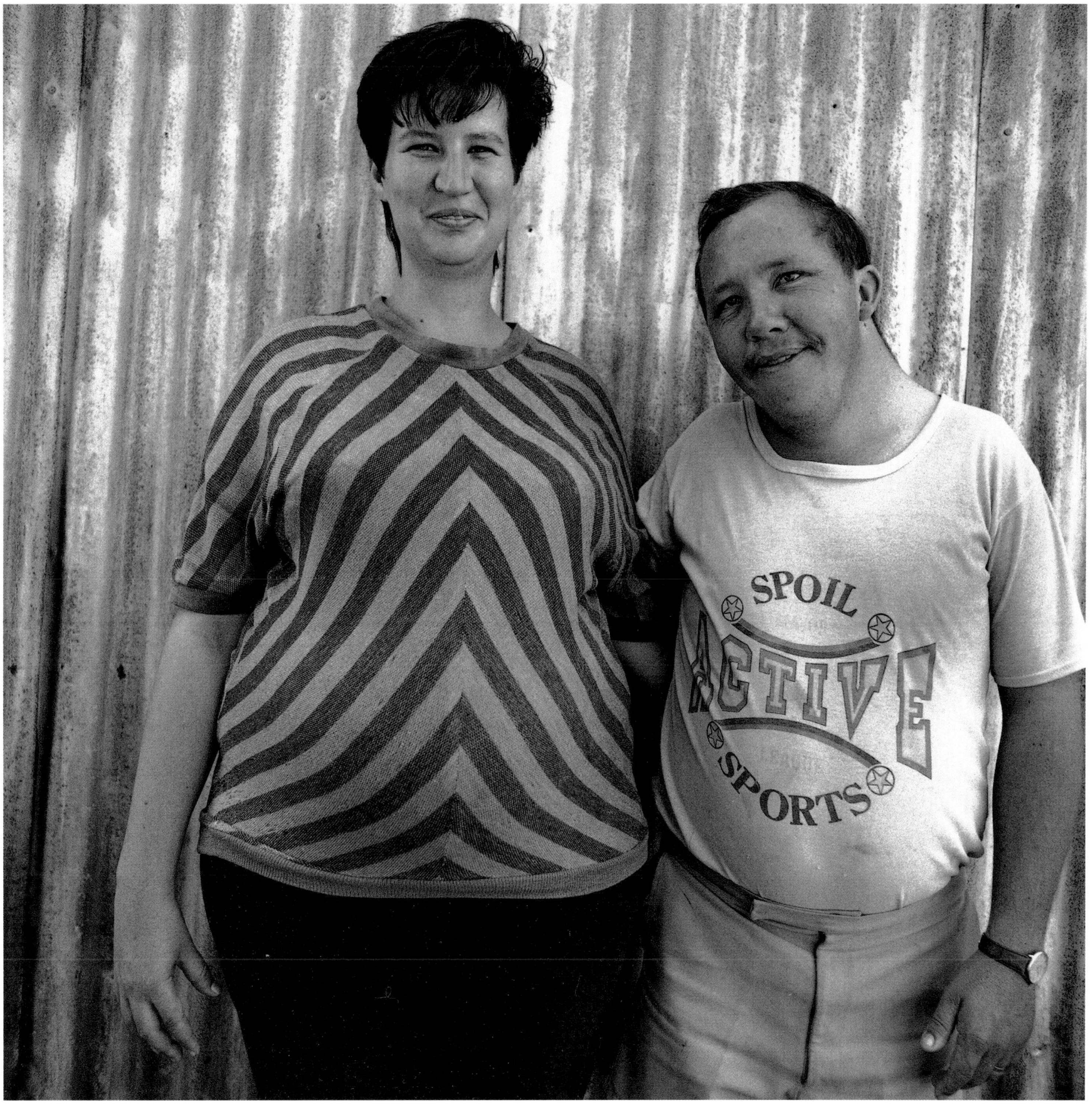
SPOIL
ACTIVE
SPORTS

Wife and daughter of ostrich farmer, Eastern Cape, 1990

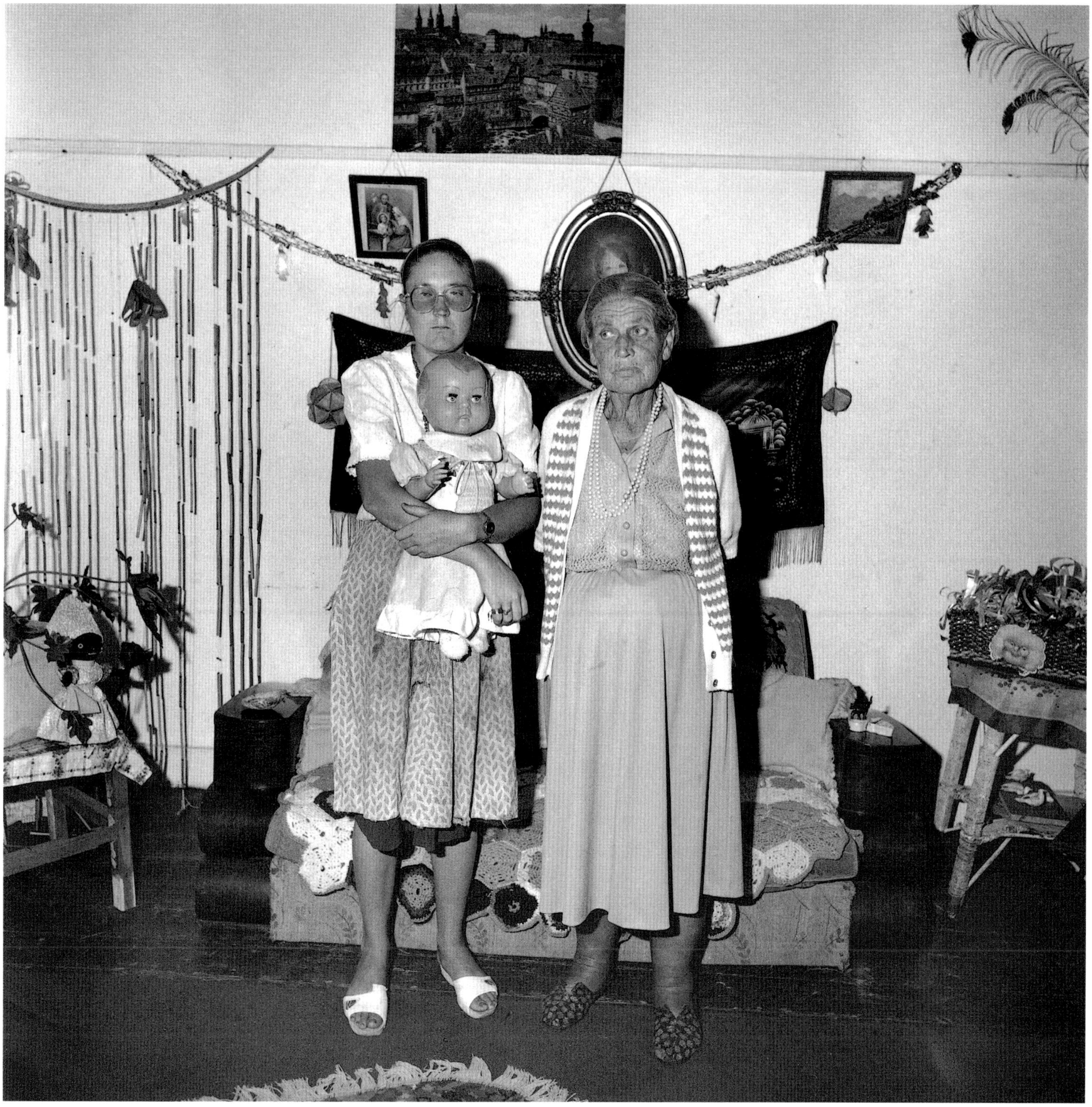

Ex-Johannesburg couple in farmhouse kitchen,
Orange Free State, 1991

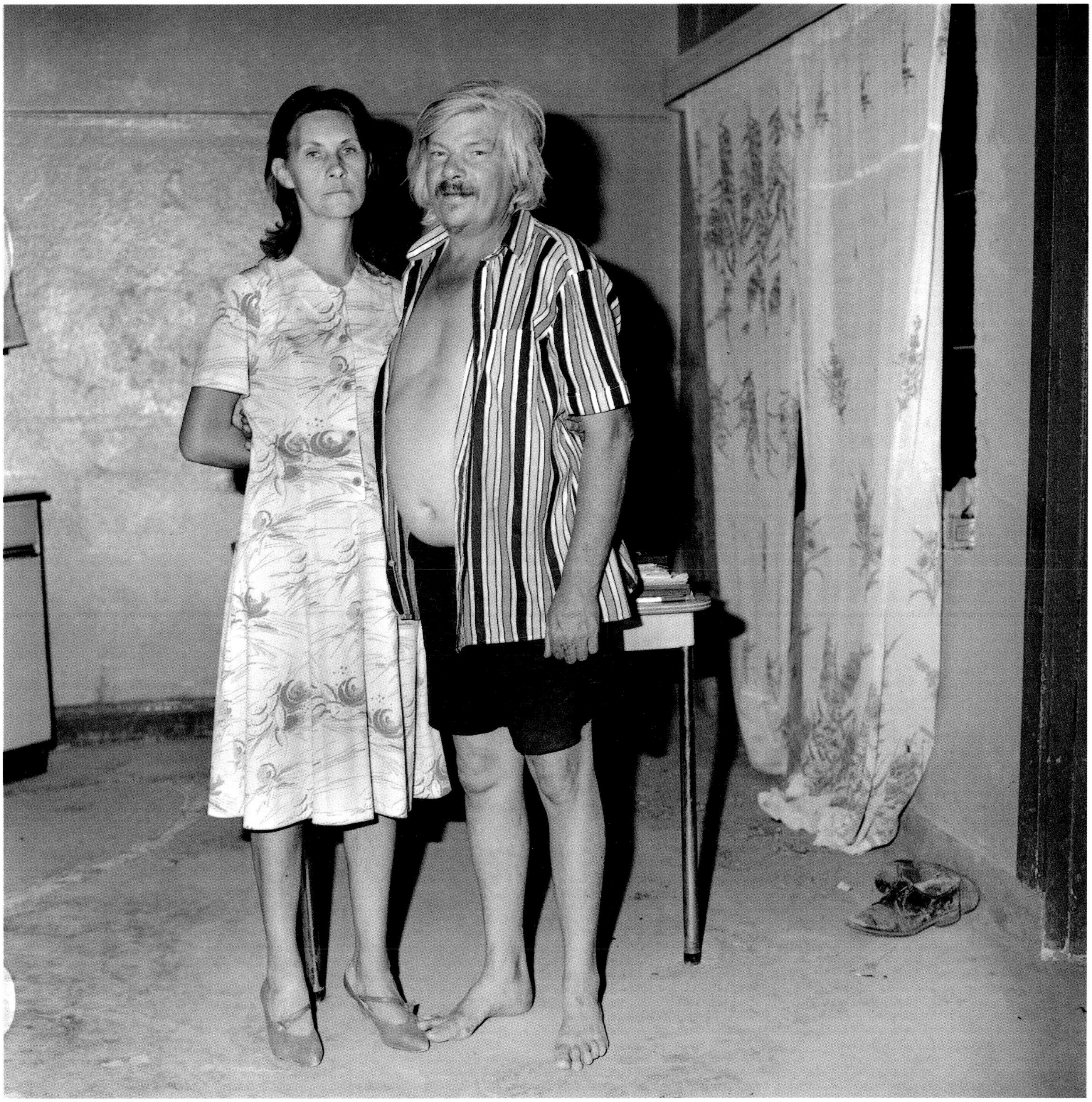

Meisie with daughters in bedroom, Southern Cape, 1991

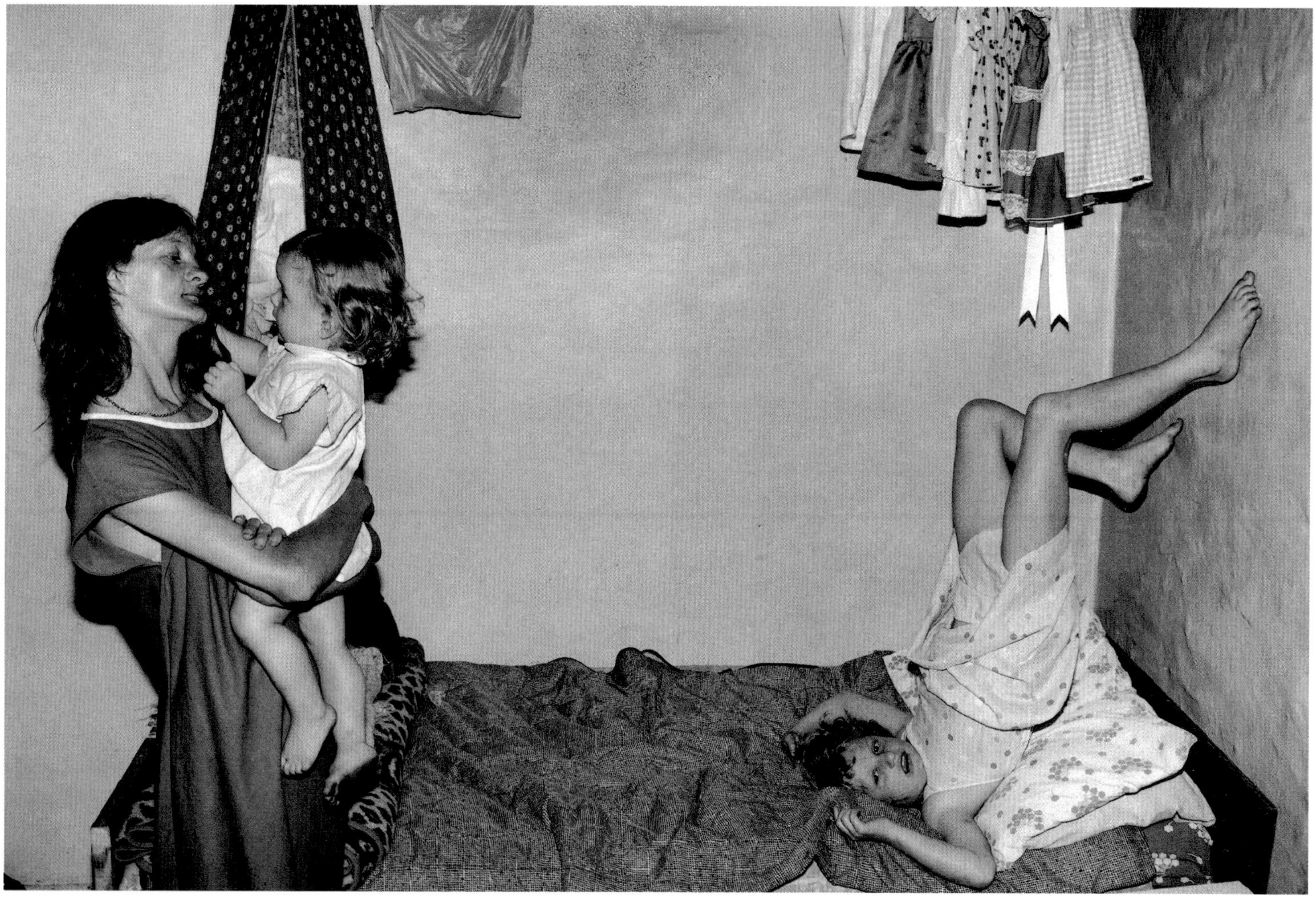

Mrs H M Cloete and neighbour, Bettie, in living room,
Orange Free State, 1992

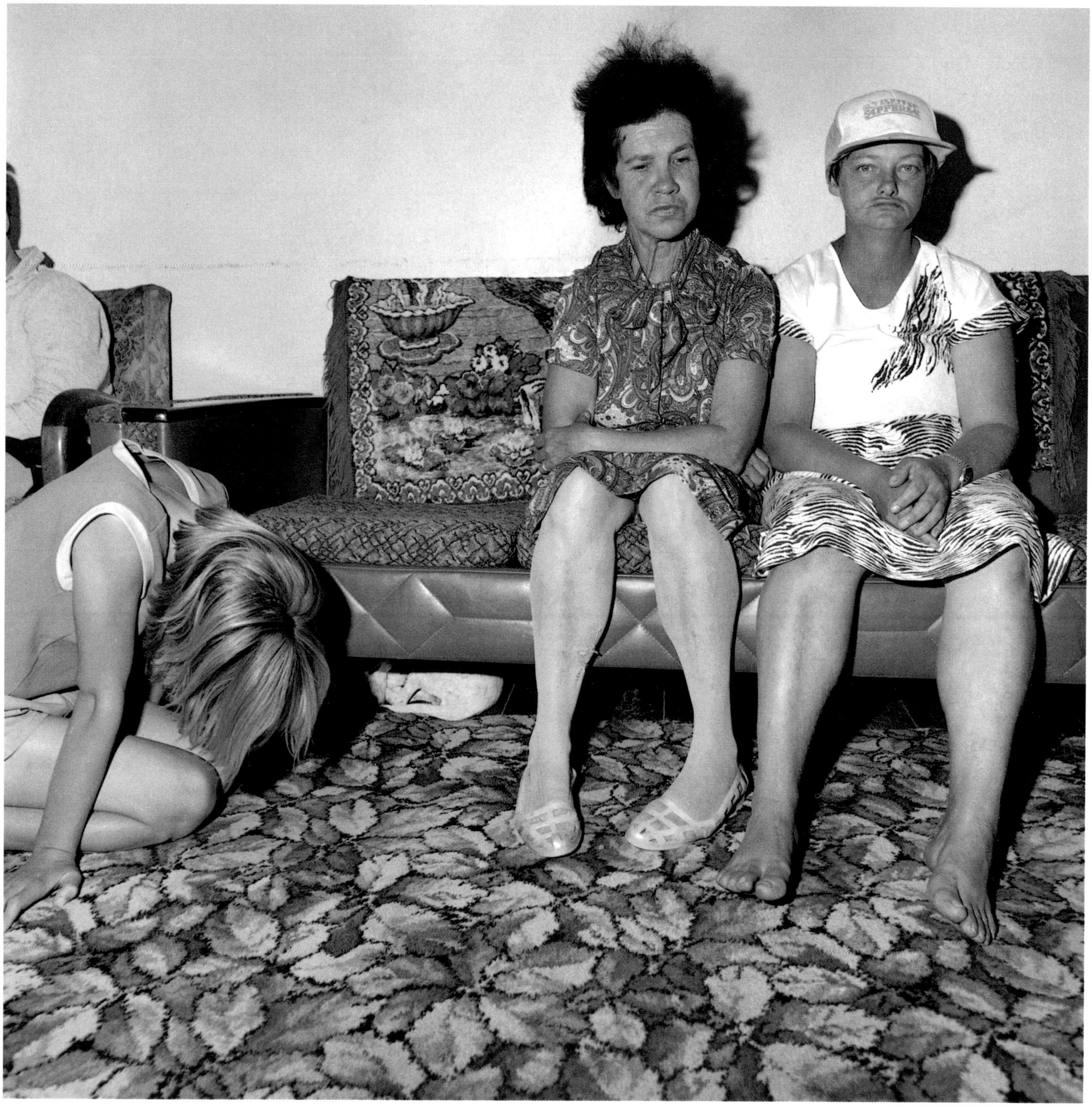

Wife of abattoir worker holding three puppies,
Orange Free State 1994

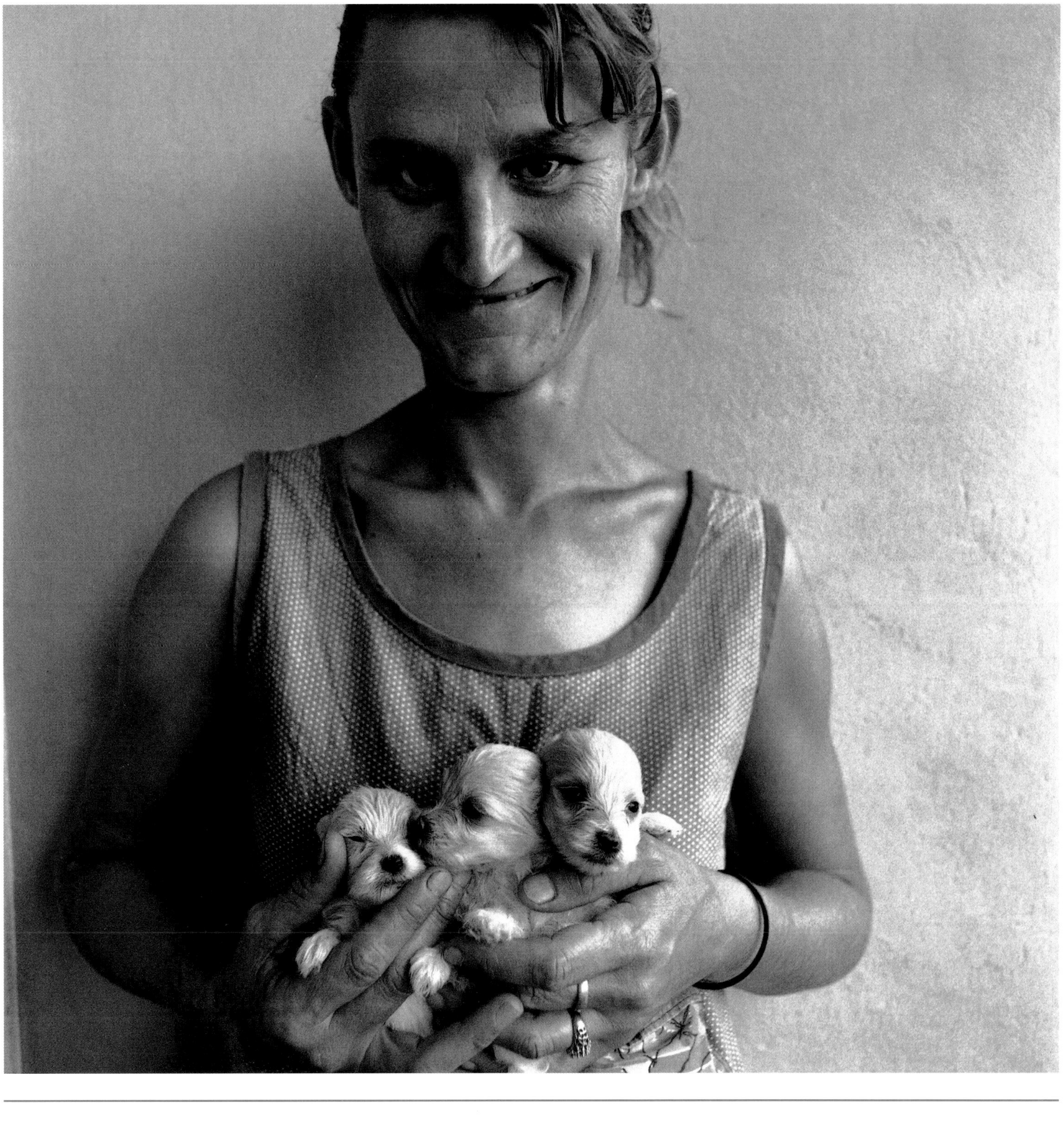

Nellie van Zyl with children,
Northern Natal, 1992

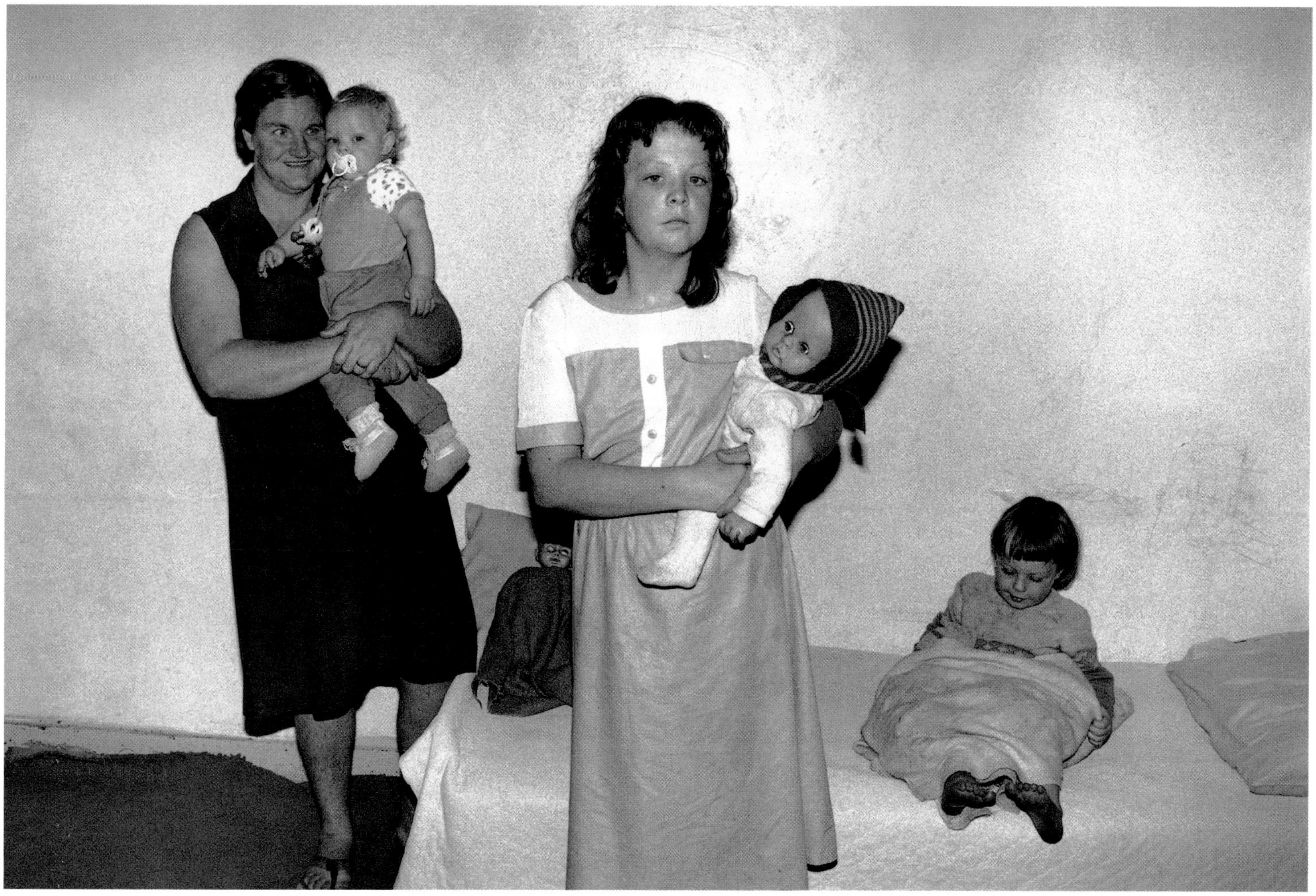

Man from platteland at girlfriend's house in city, Central Transvaal, 1988

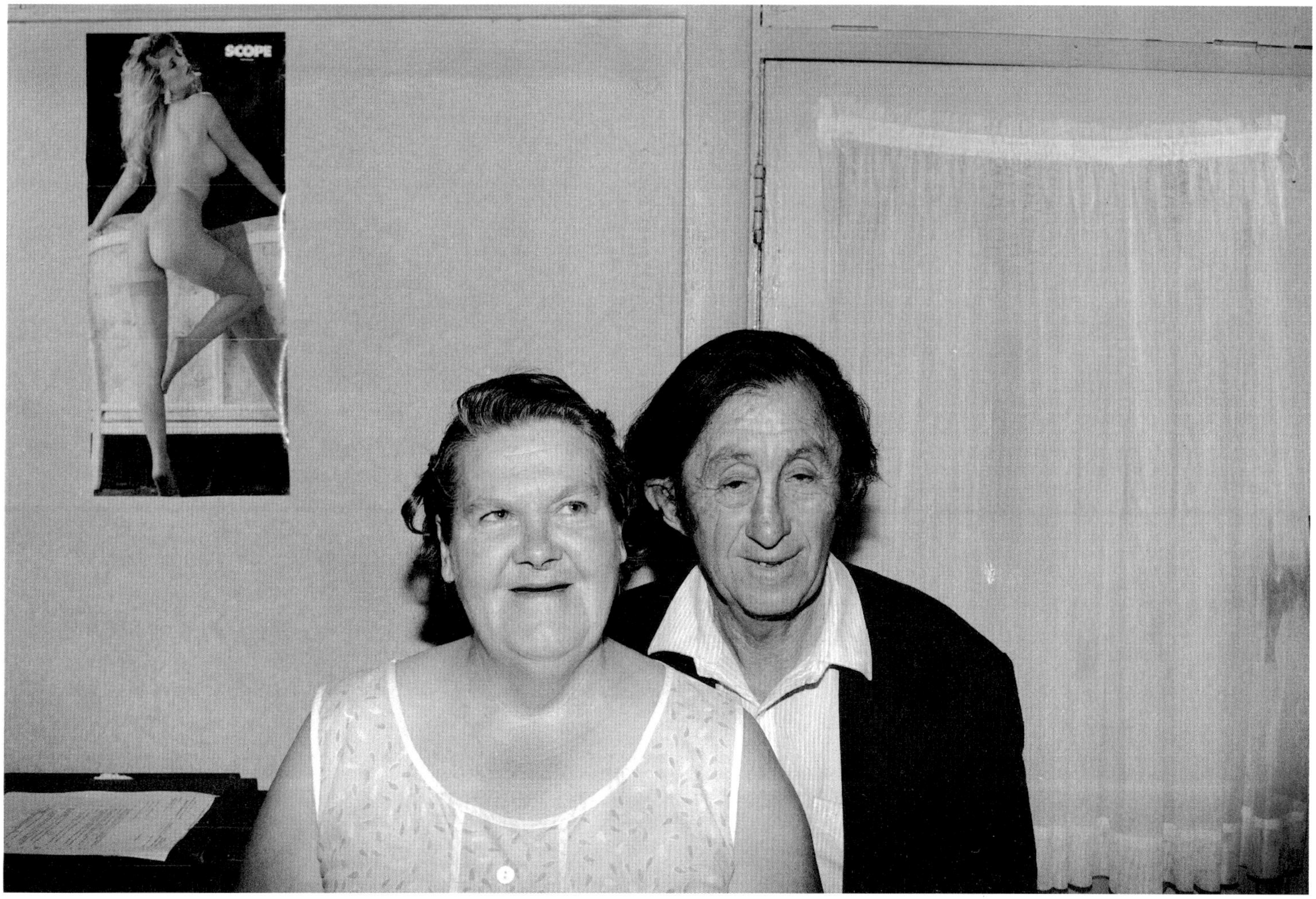
SCOPE

Leah and Illona, sisters, Western Transvaal, 1986

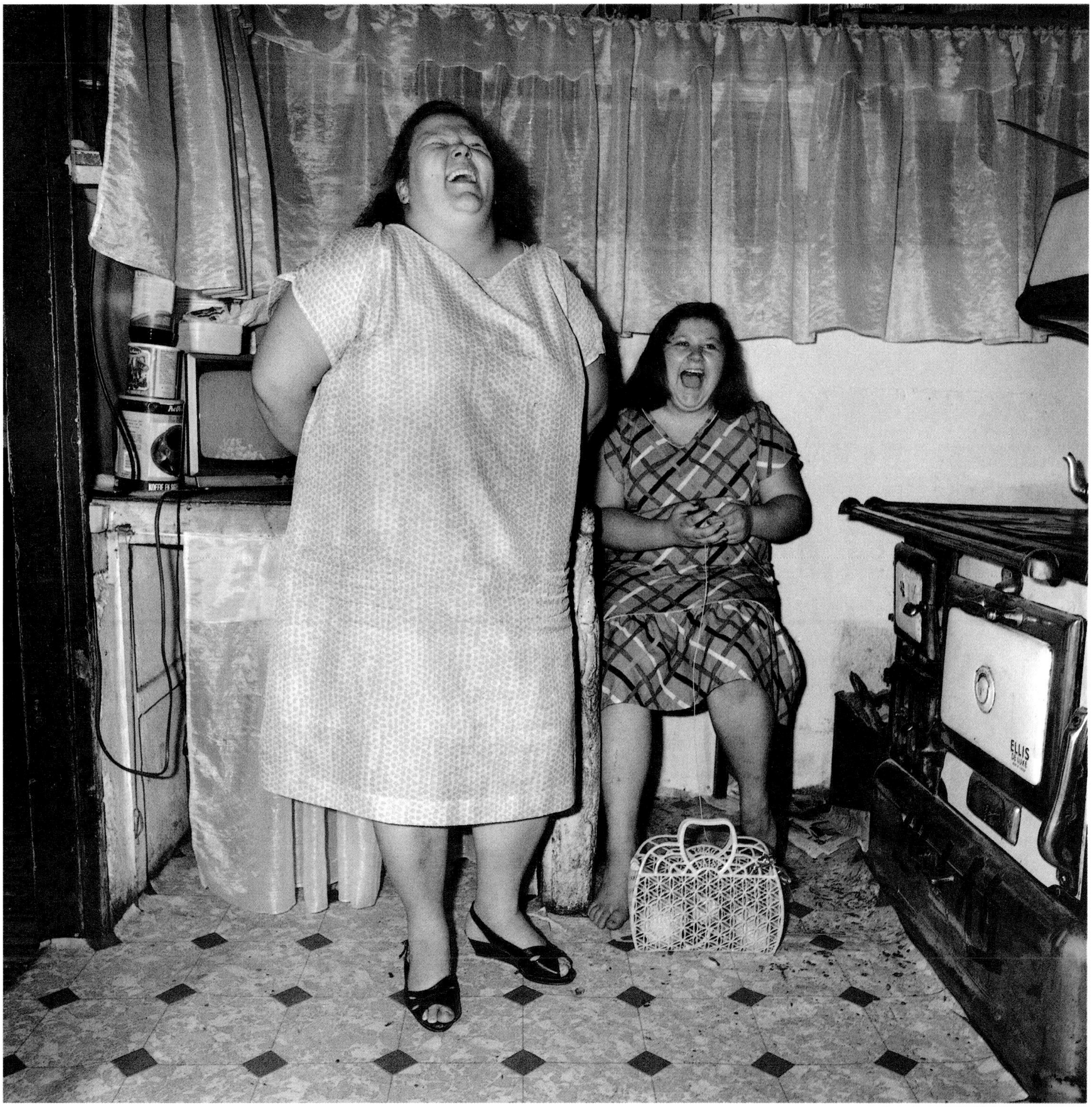
ELLIS

Diamond digger and son standing on bed, Western Transvaal, 1987

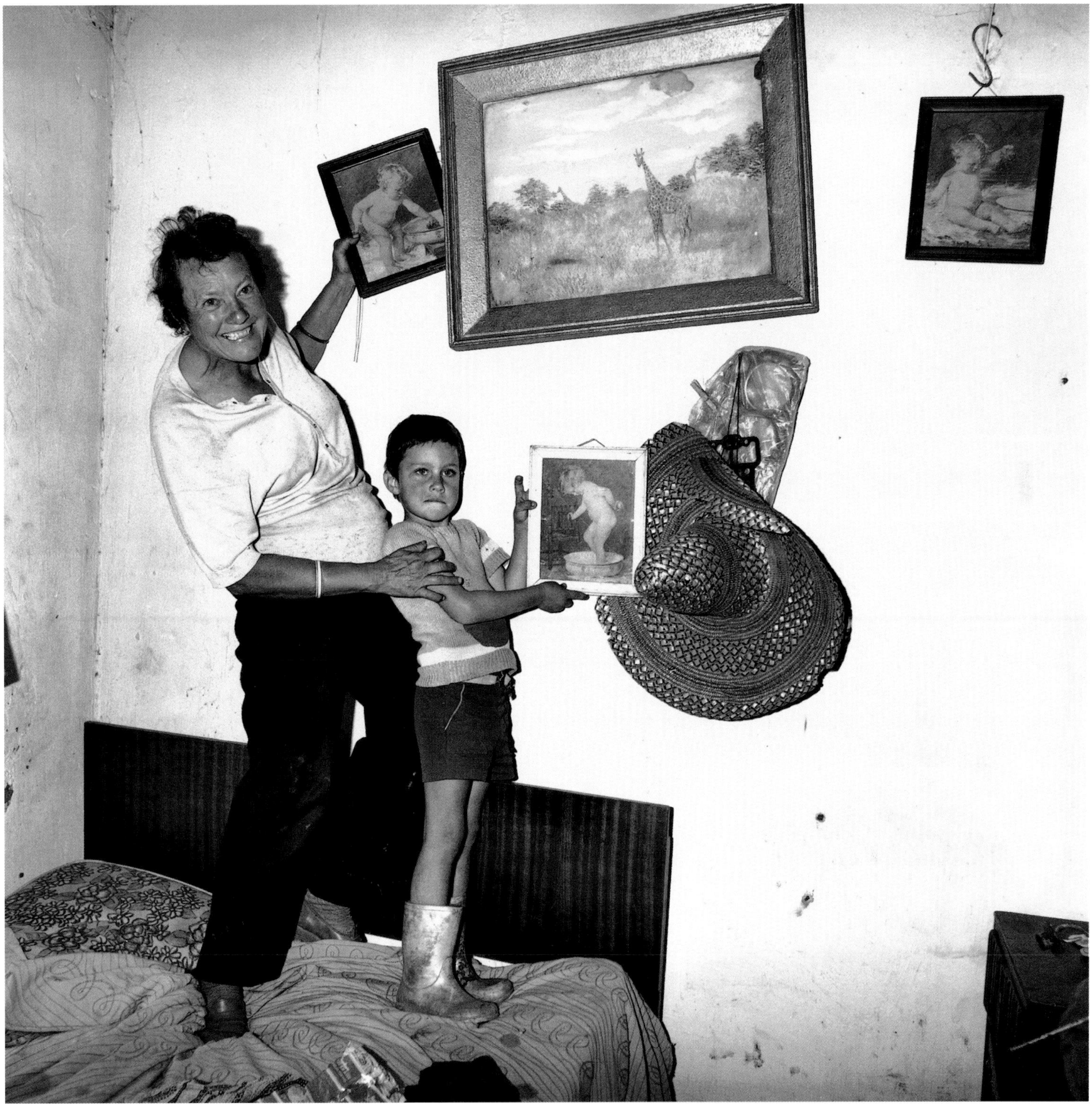

Teenager with glass eye, Western Transvaal, 1994

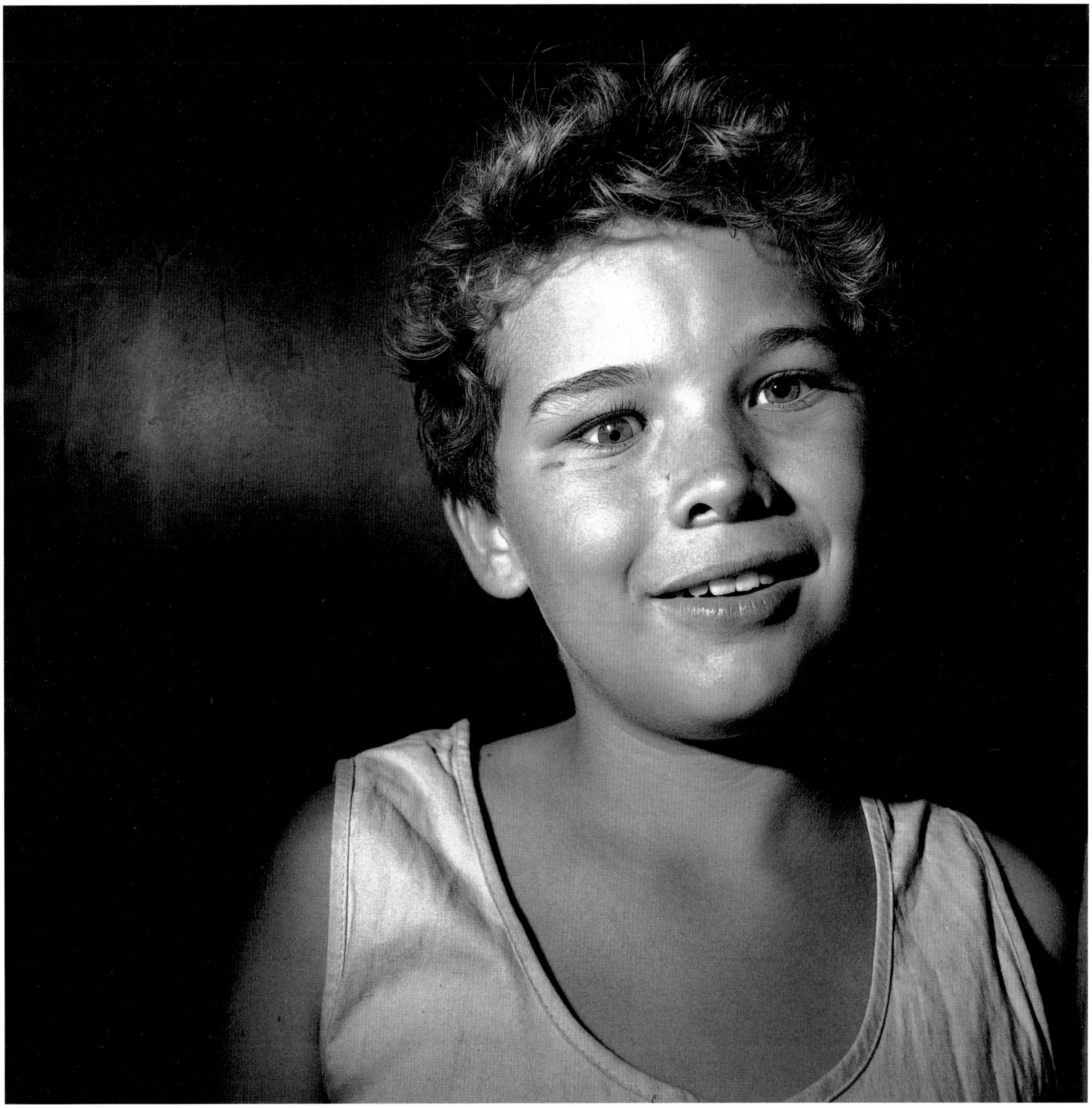

Unemployed youth with sister, Western Transvaal, 1991

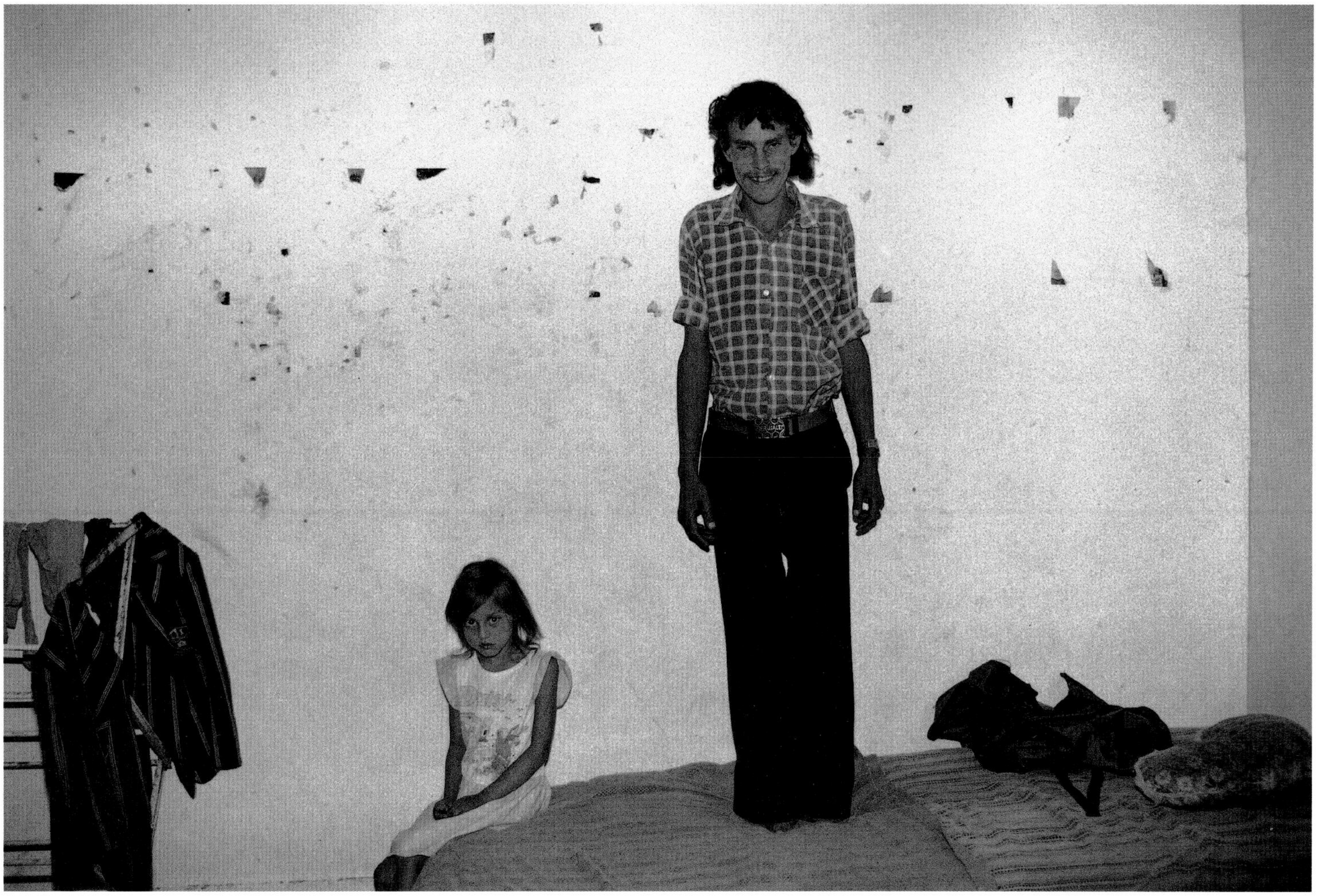

Children from countryside in city home, Central Transvaal, 1987

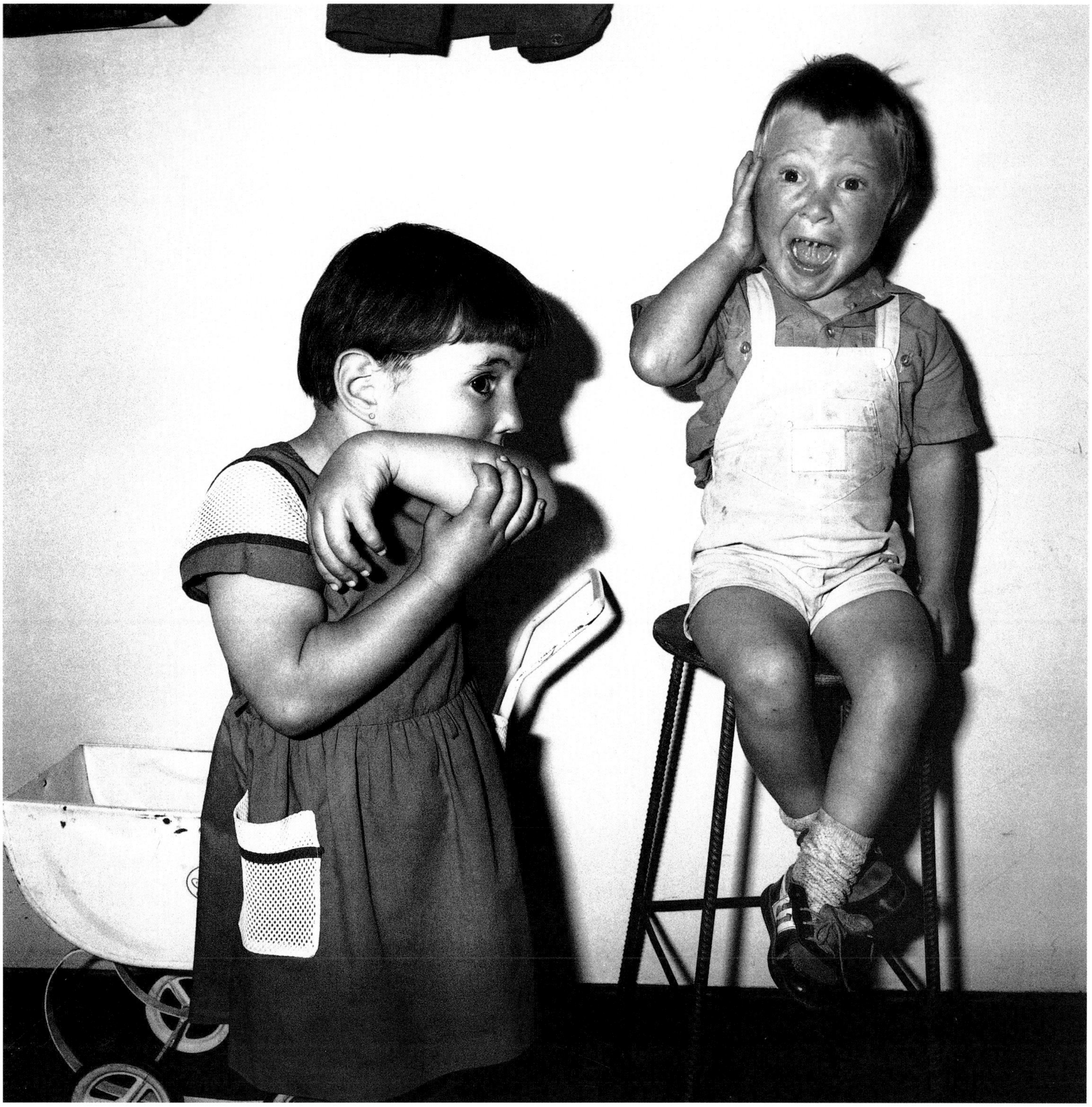

Wife of transporter with children,
Orange Free State, 1990

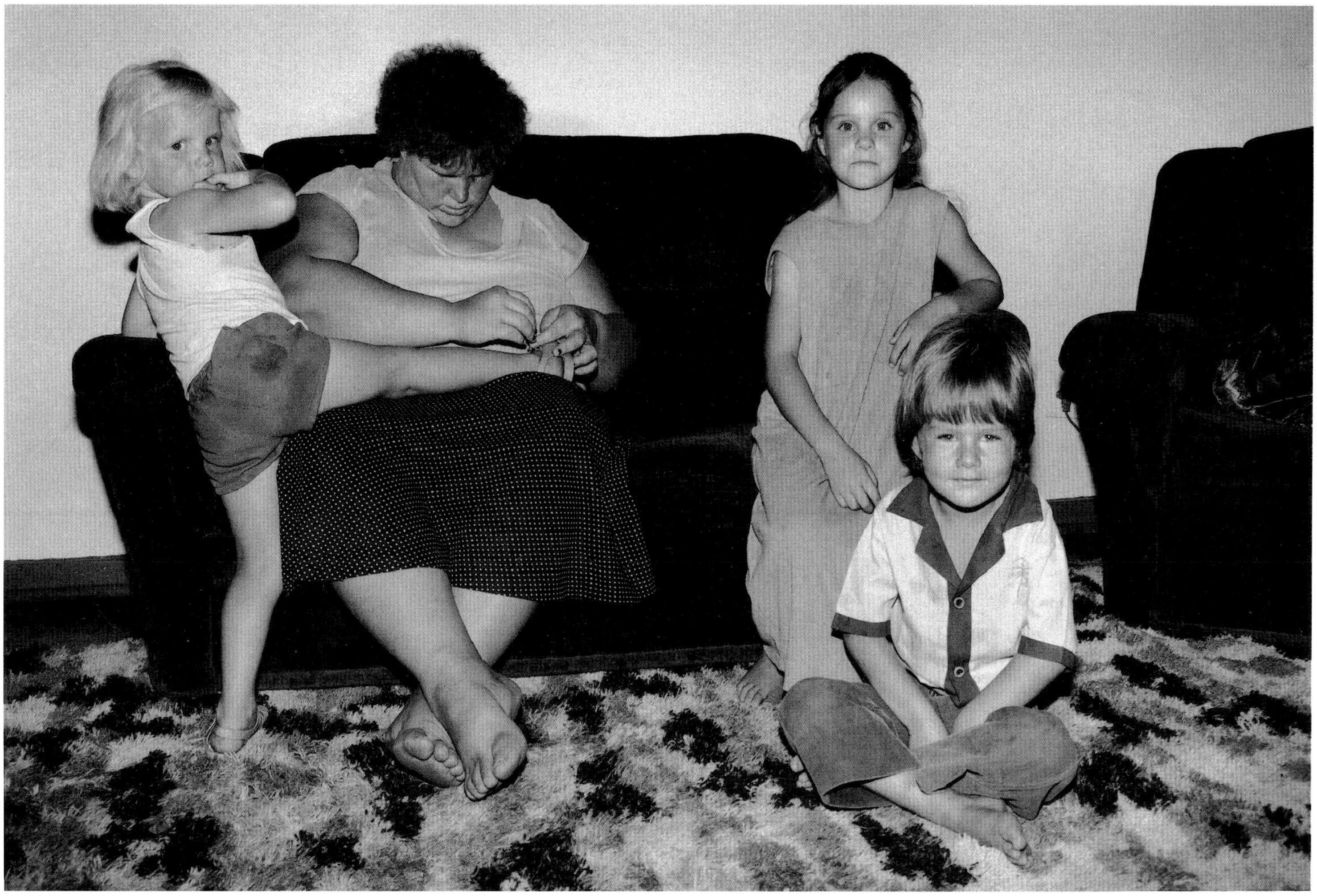

Apricot farmer and wife, Southern Cape, 1993

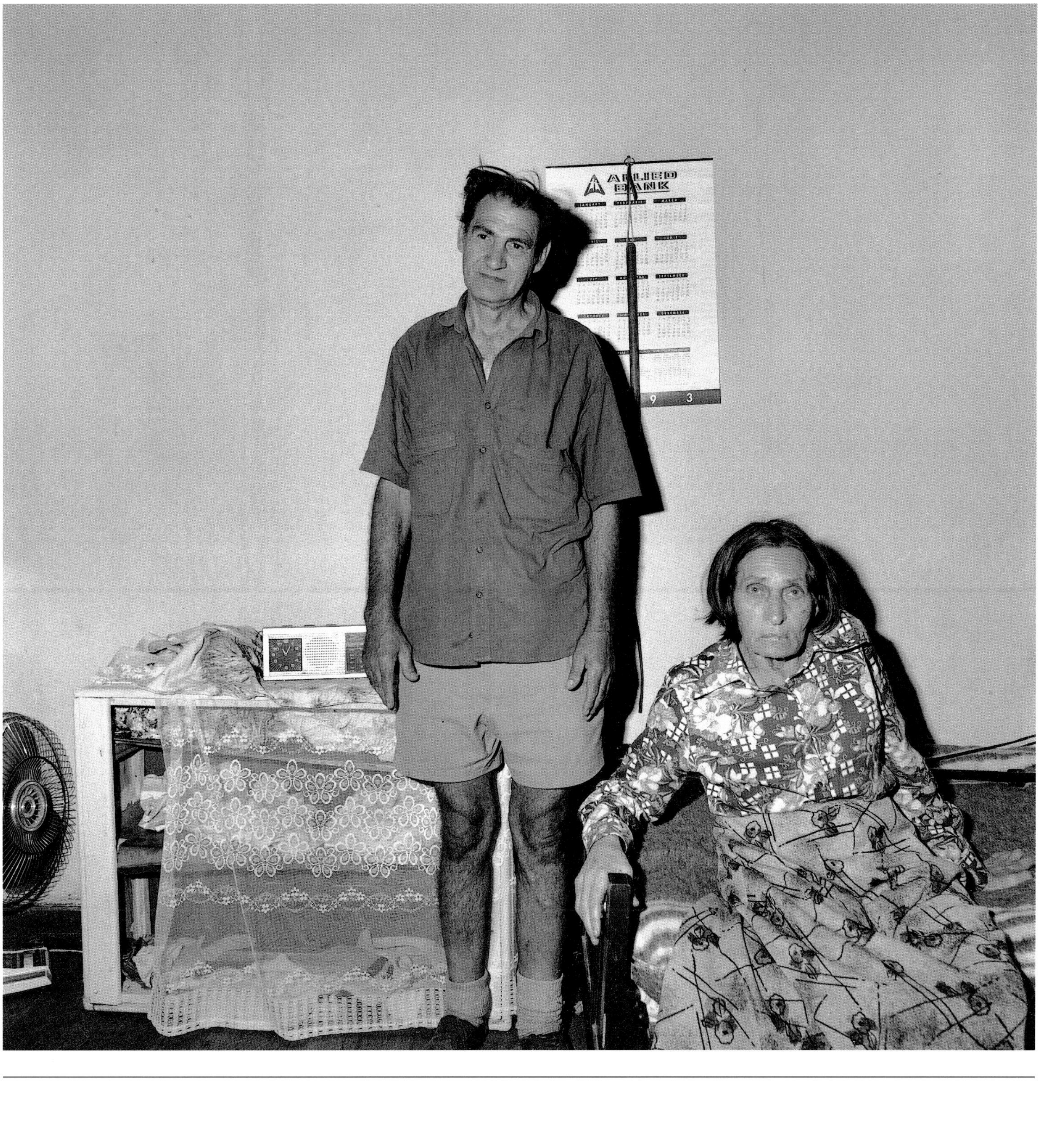
ALLIED
BANK
JANUARY
MARCH
JUNIE
JULY
SEPTEMBER
DESEMBER
9 3

Man with mother and child, Northern Cape, 1991

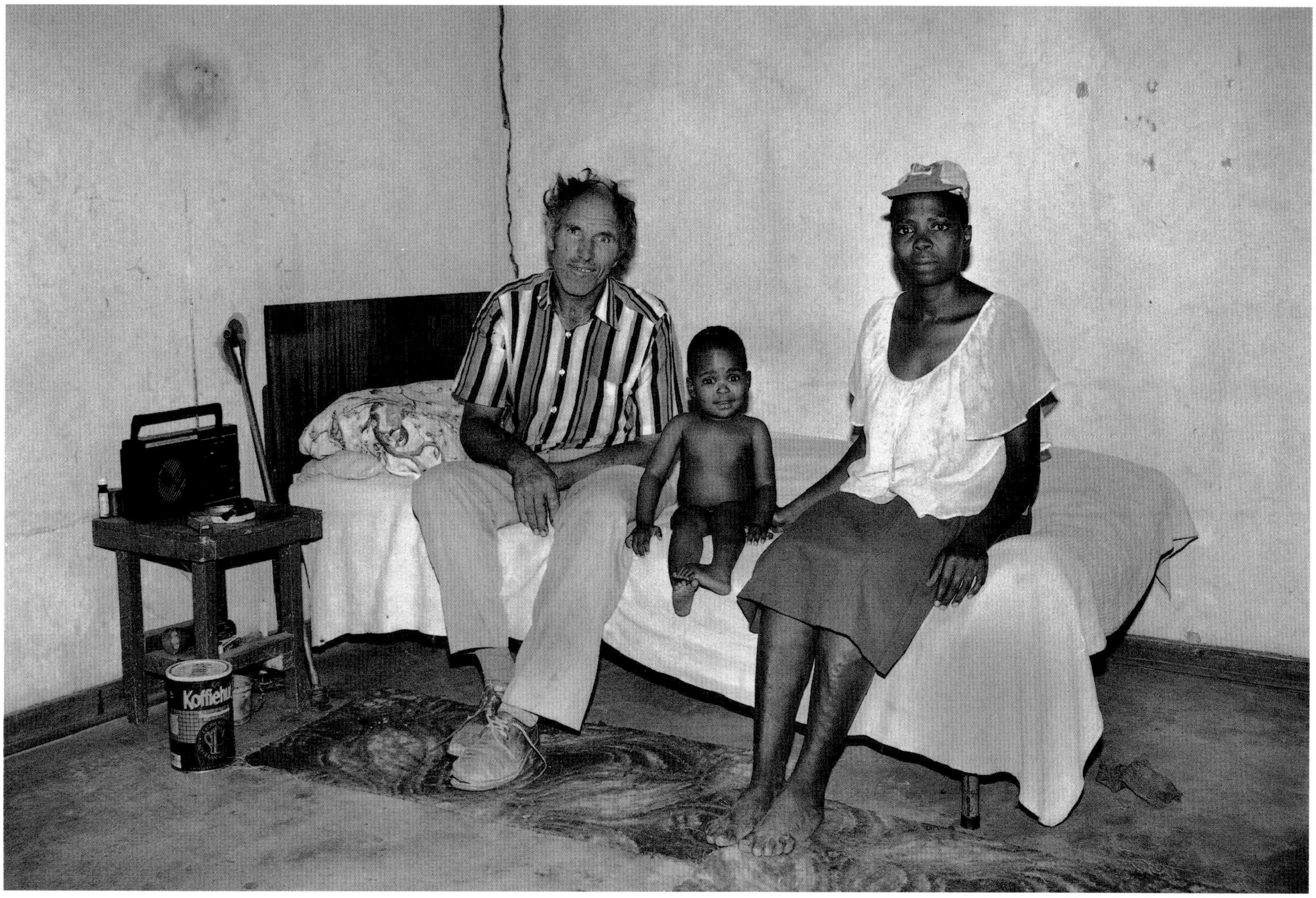

Wessie du Plessis, delivery boy, holding white kitten, Eastern Cape,1994

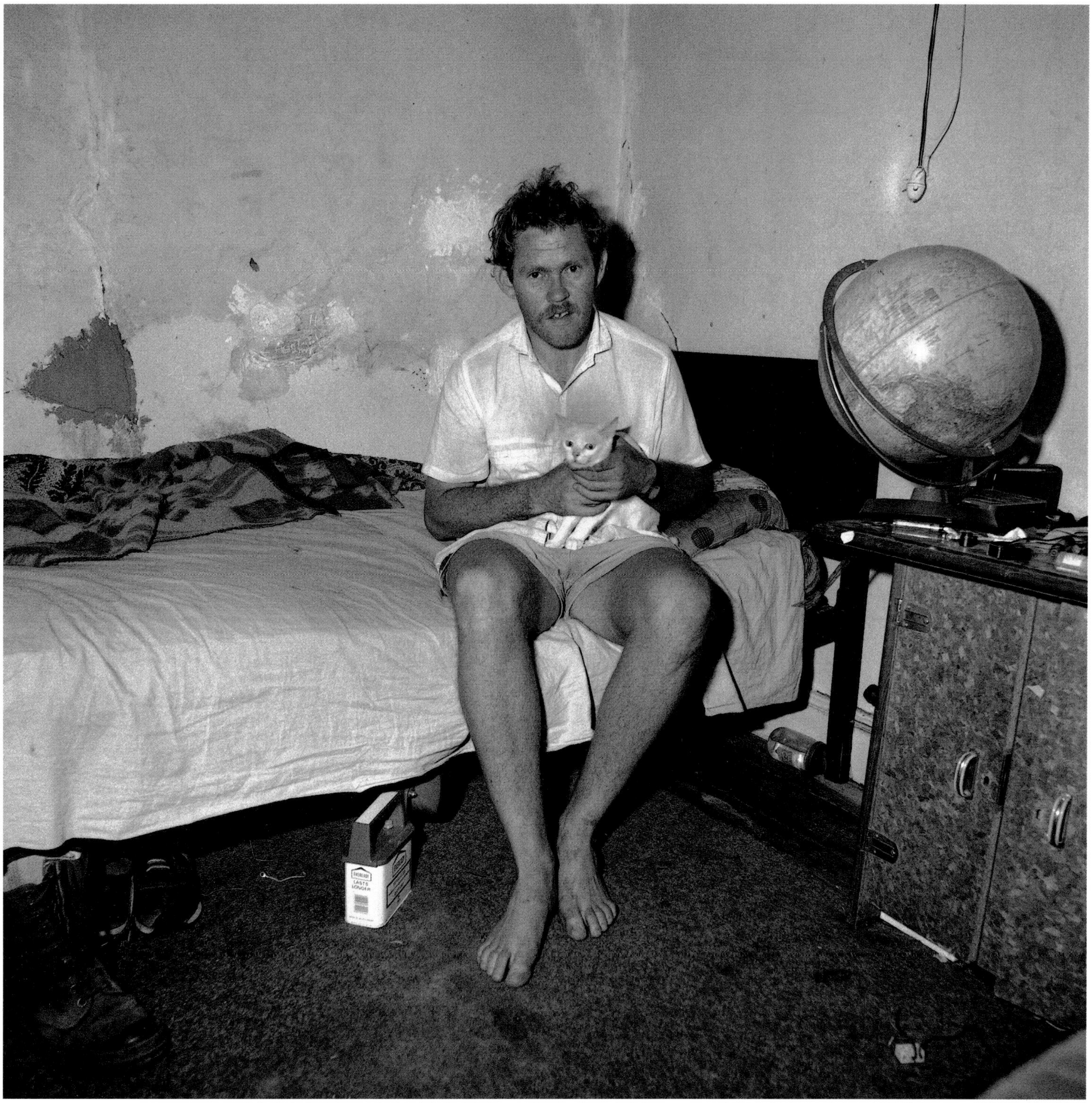
LASTS
LONGER

Man and woman in boarding house,
Western Transvaal, 1992

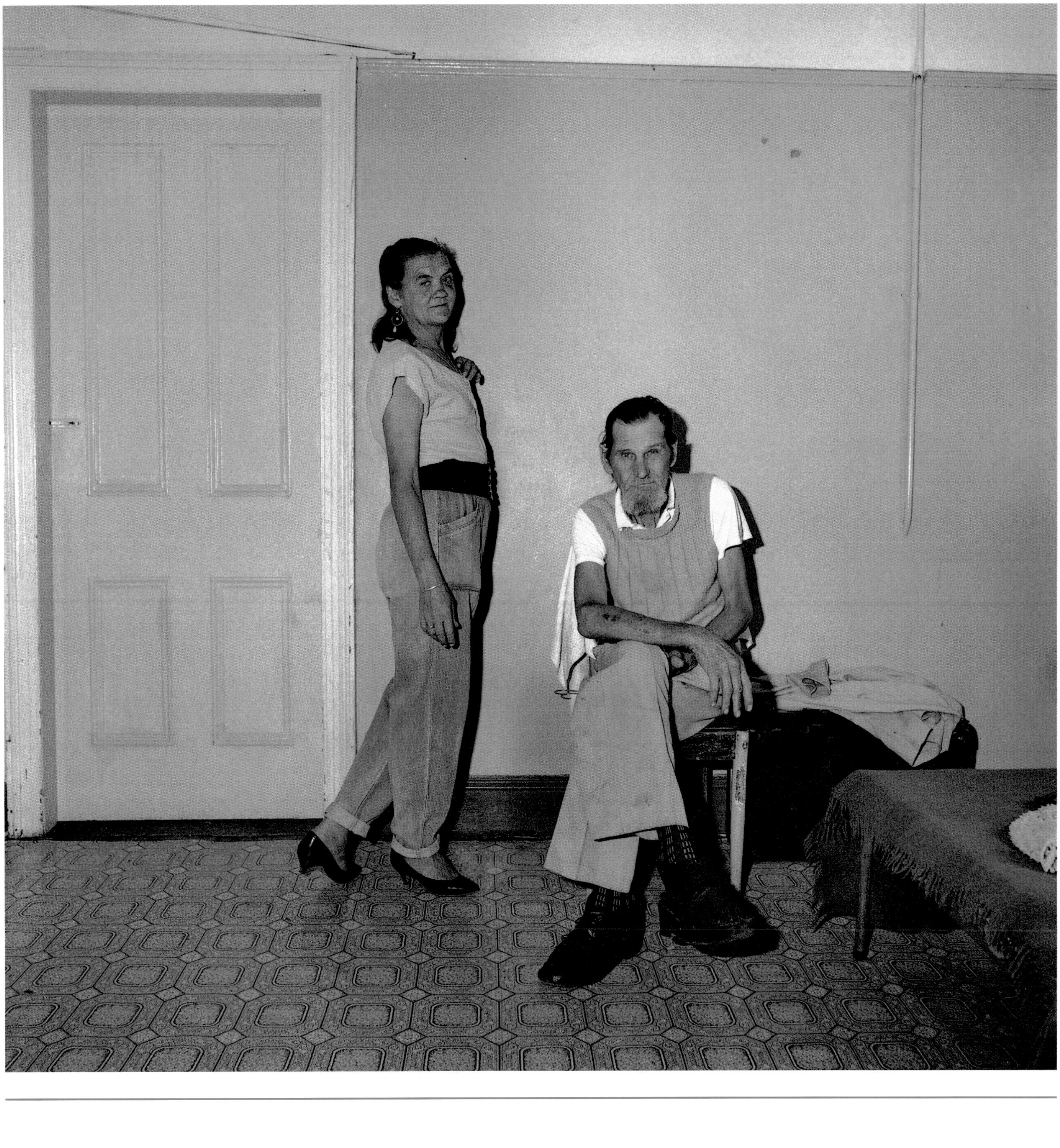

Ex-big-gamehunter and wife, Western Transvaal, 1987

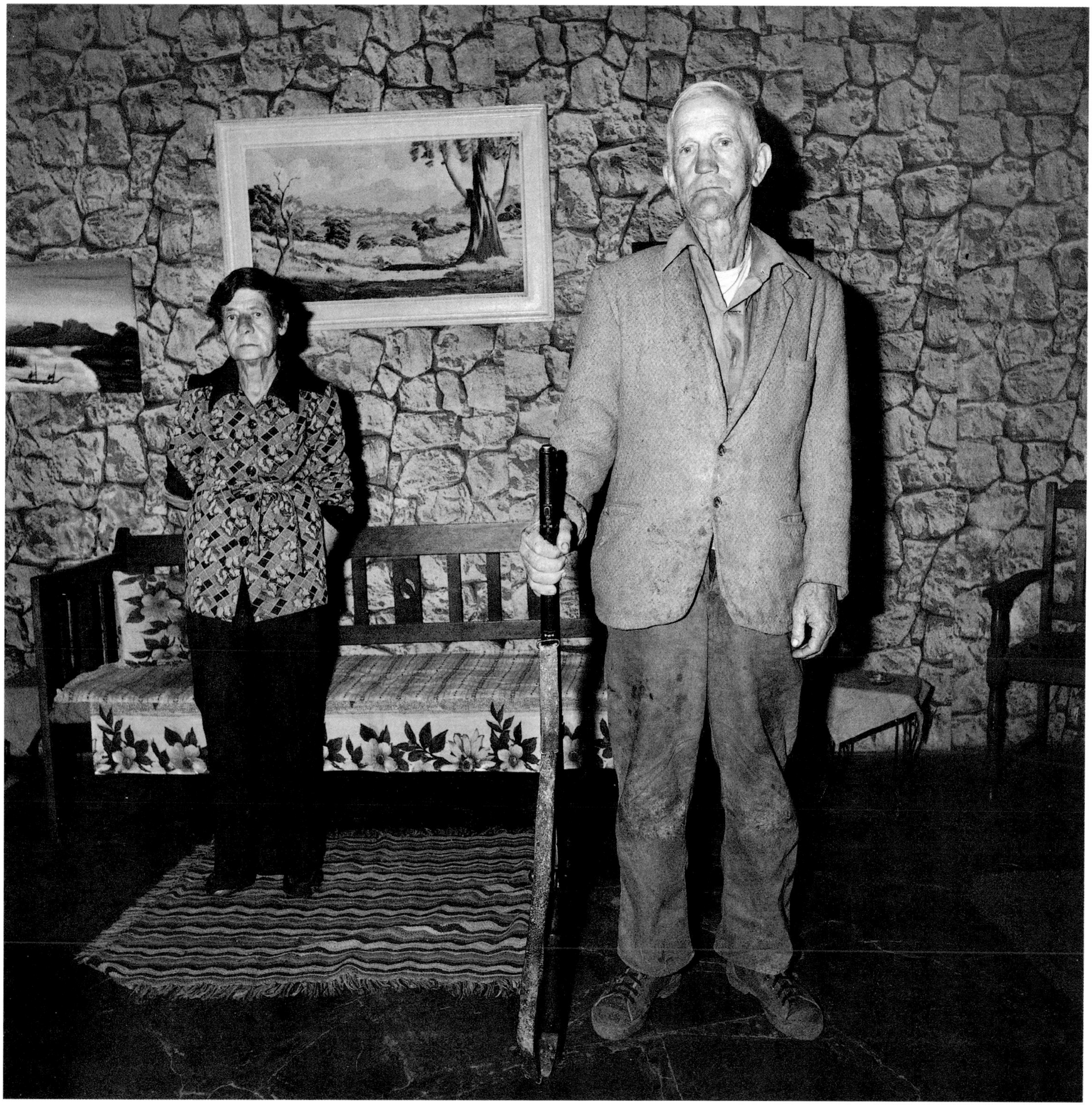

Cookie with wife, Tillie, Orange Free State, 1993

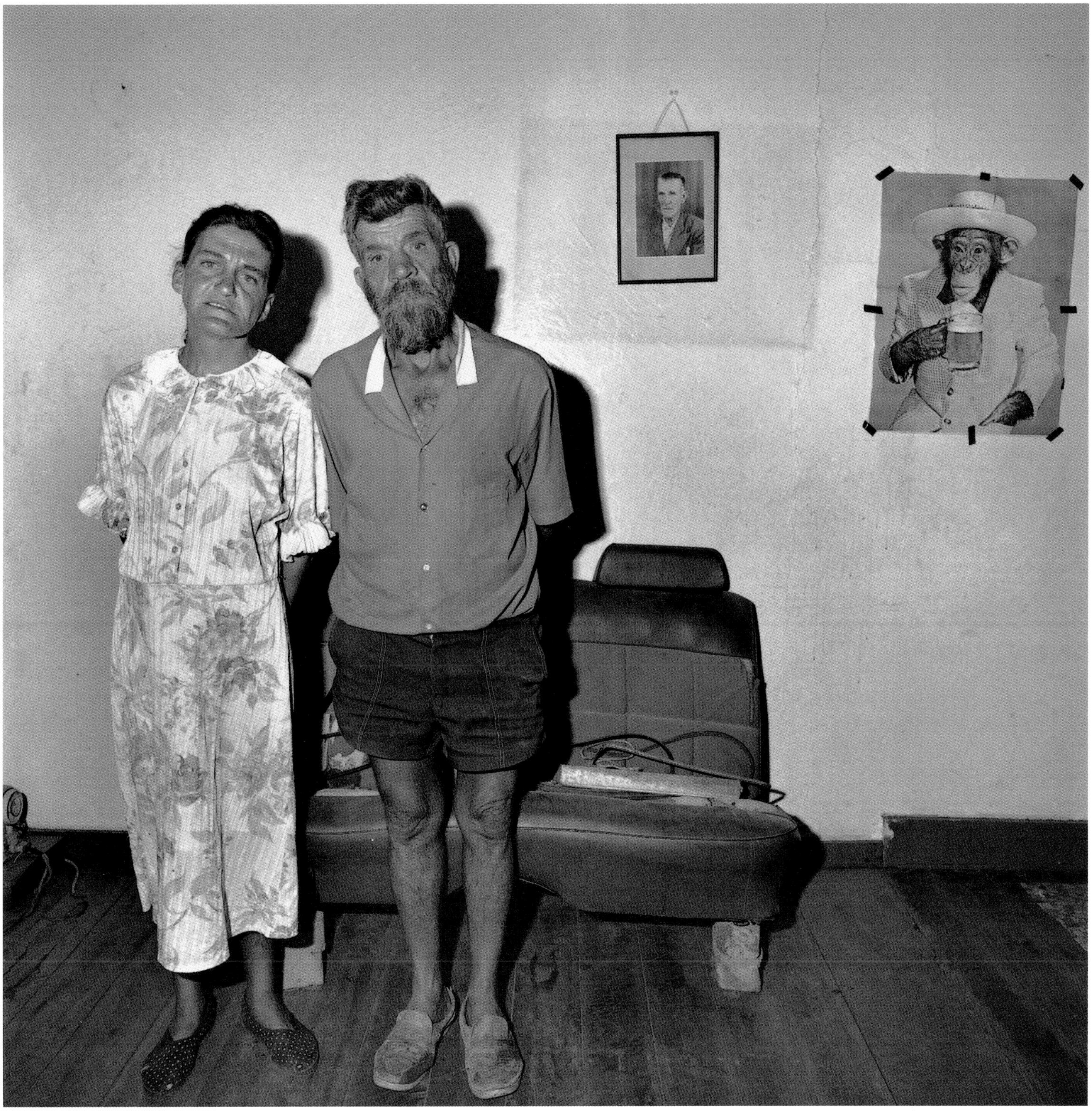

J T Terreblanche with mother, Western Transvaal, 1990

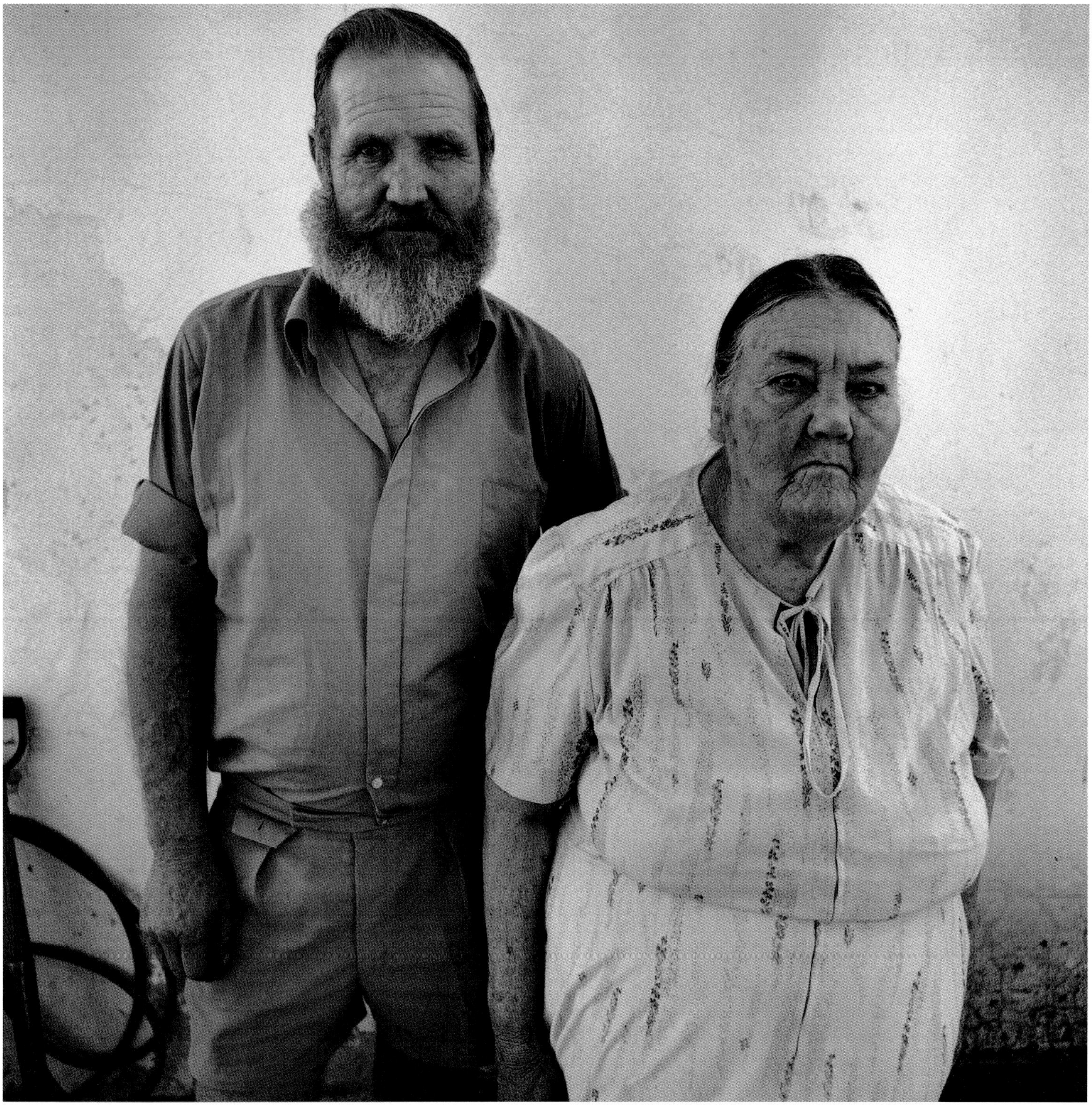

Man on front verandah, Southern Transvaal, 1989

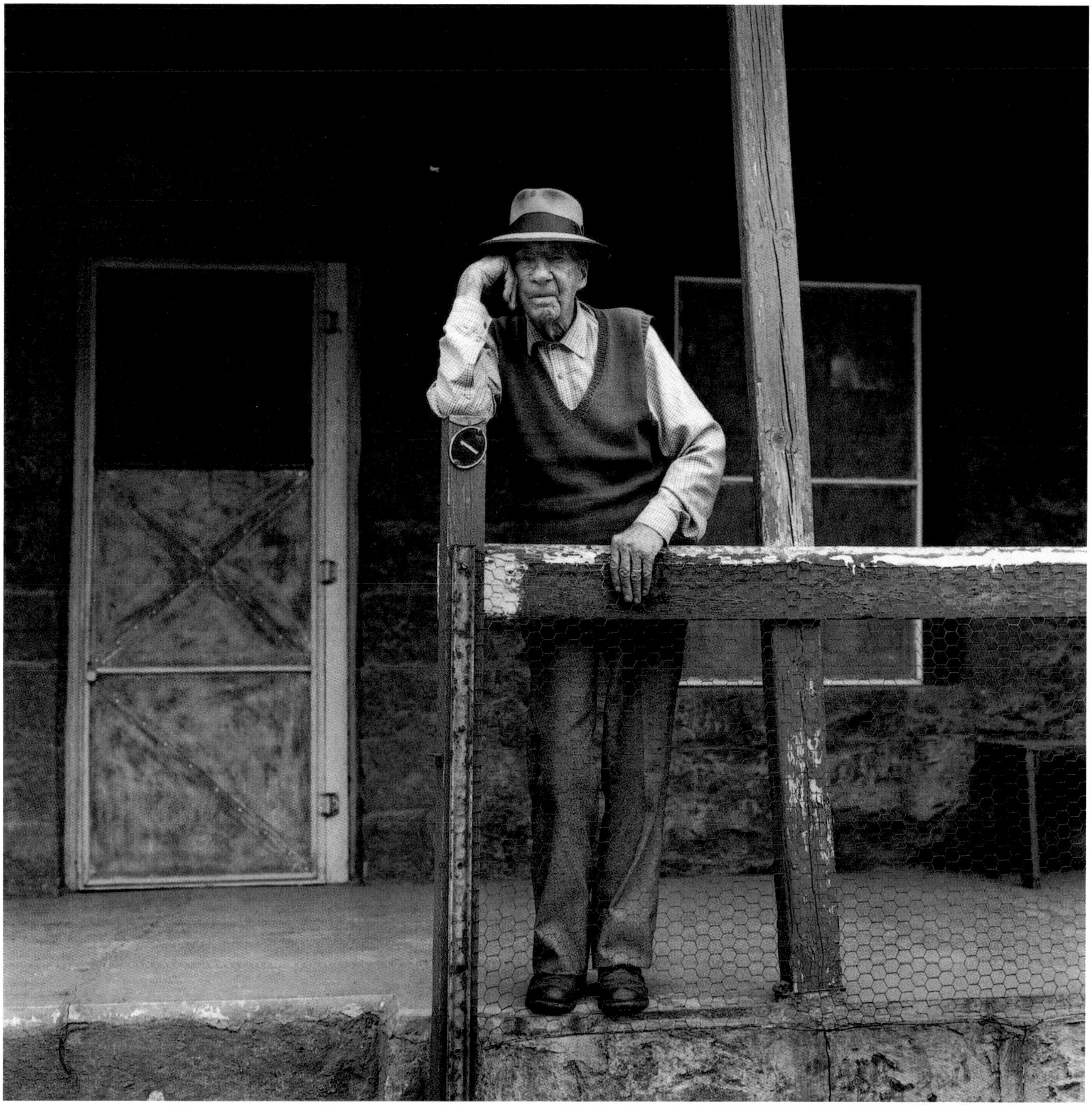

Mrs J J Joubert and dog, Dinky, in bedroom,
Central Cape, 1990

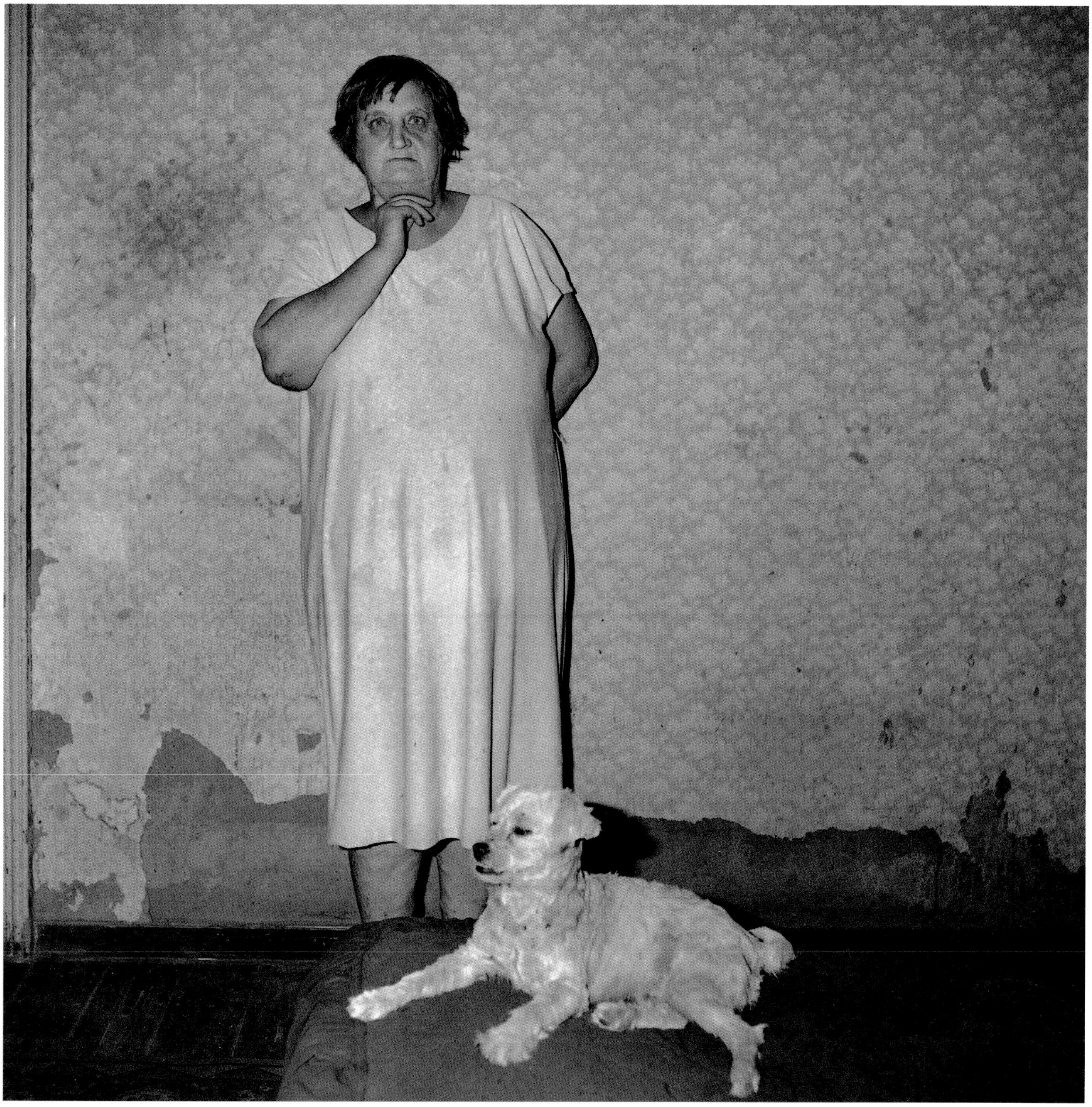

Scrapyard worker and family, Central Transvaal, 1993

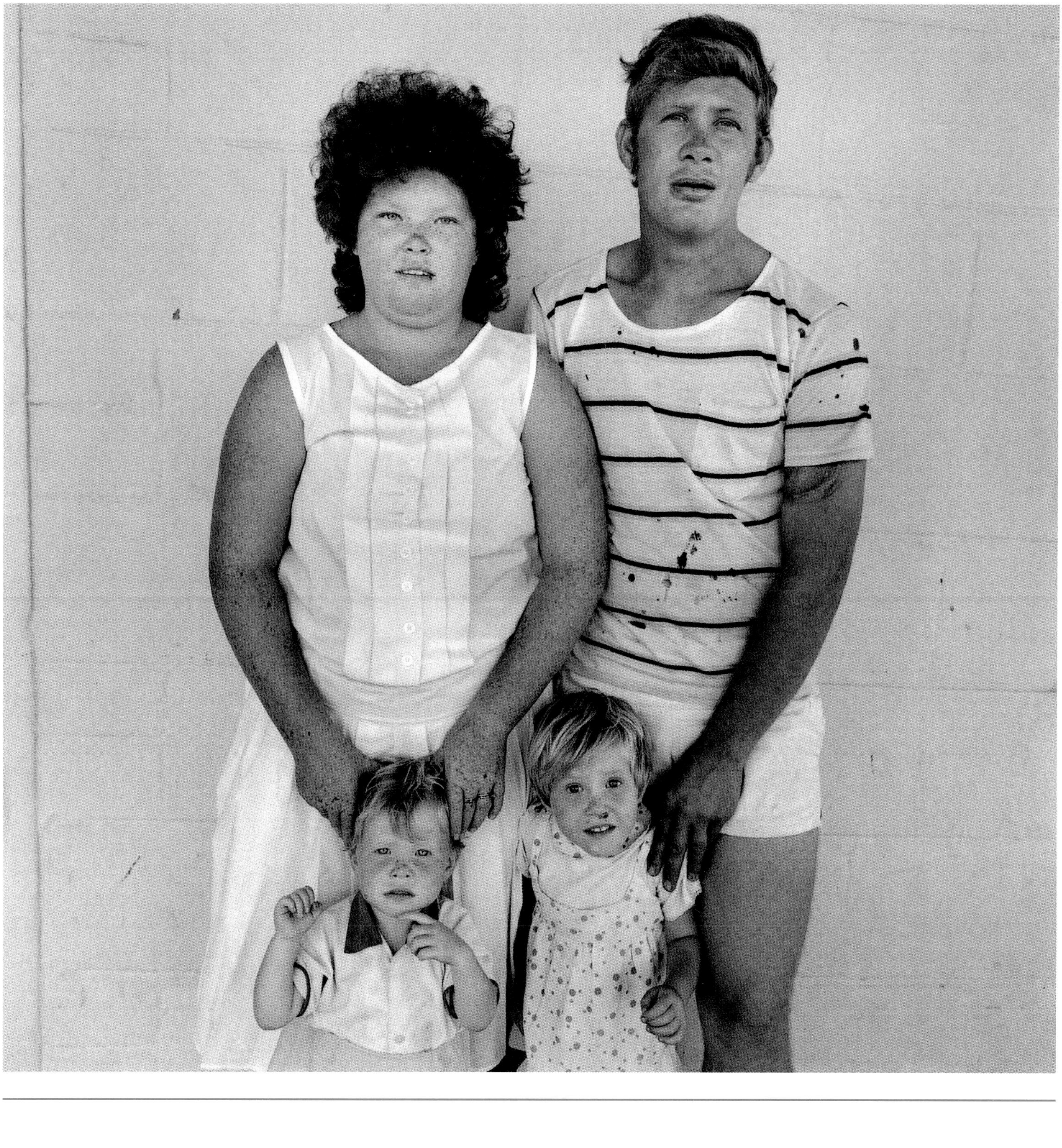

N van Wyk, evangelist, Western Transvaal, 1992

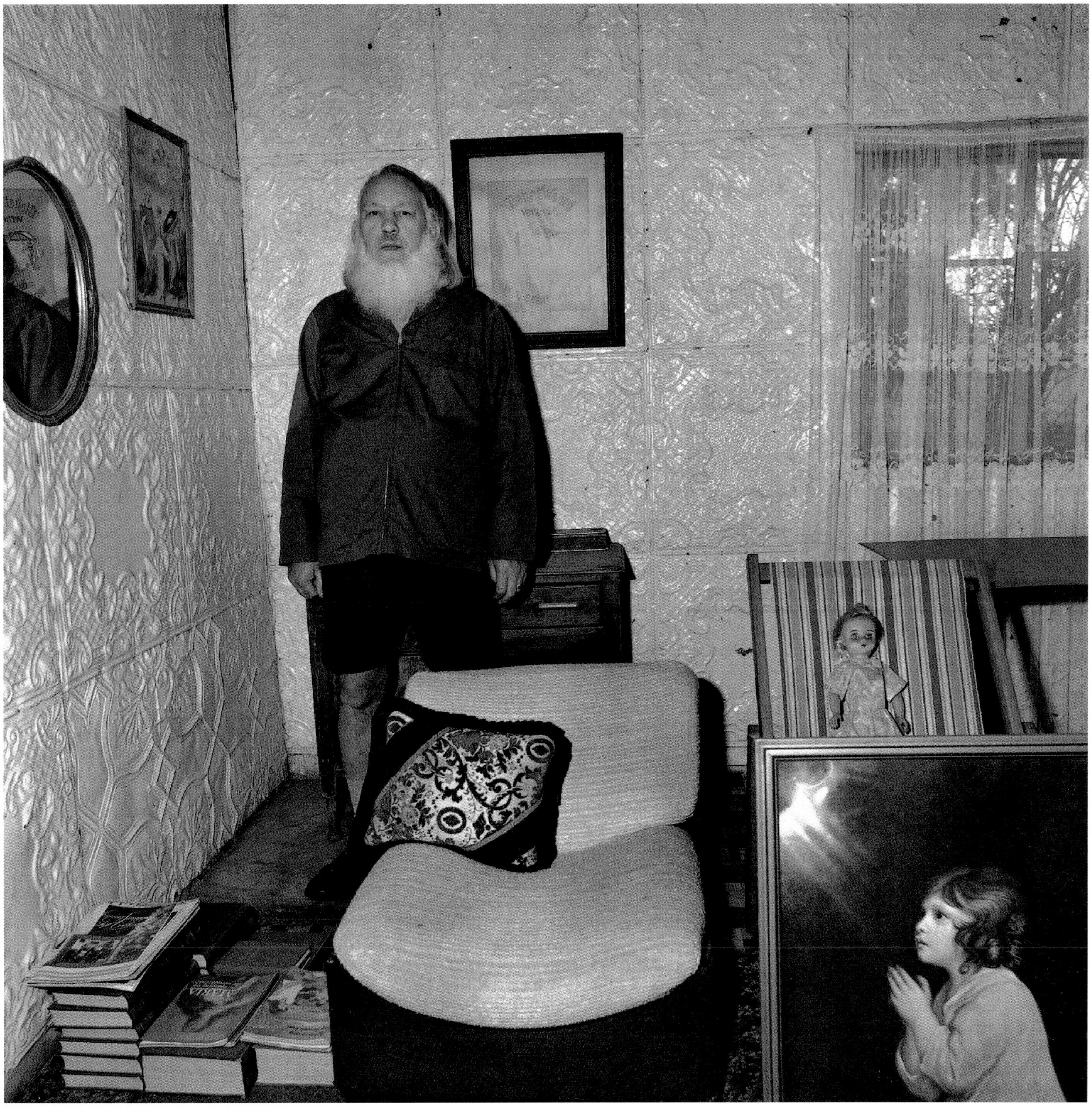

Man and maid, Northern Cape, 1991

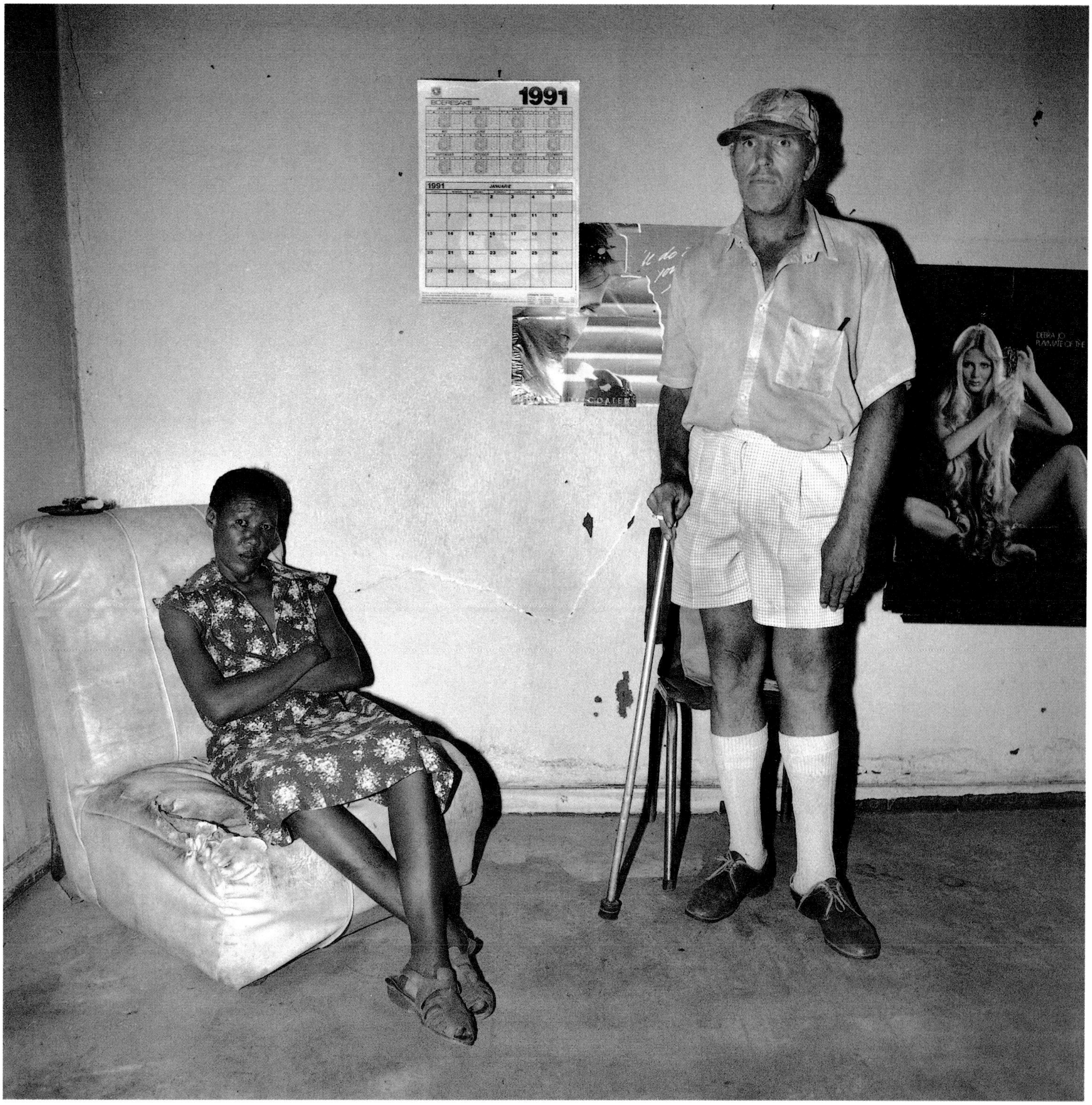
1991
BOERESAKE
1991
JANUARIE

Railwayman with wife, Annabell, and son, Petrus,
Western Transvaal, 1987

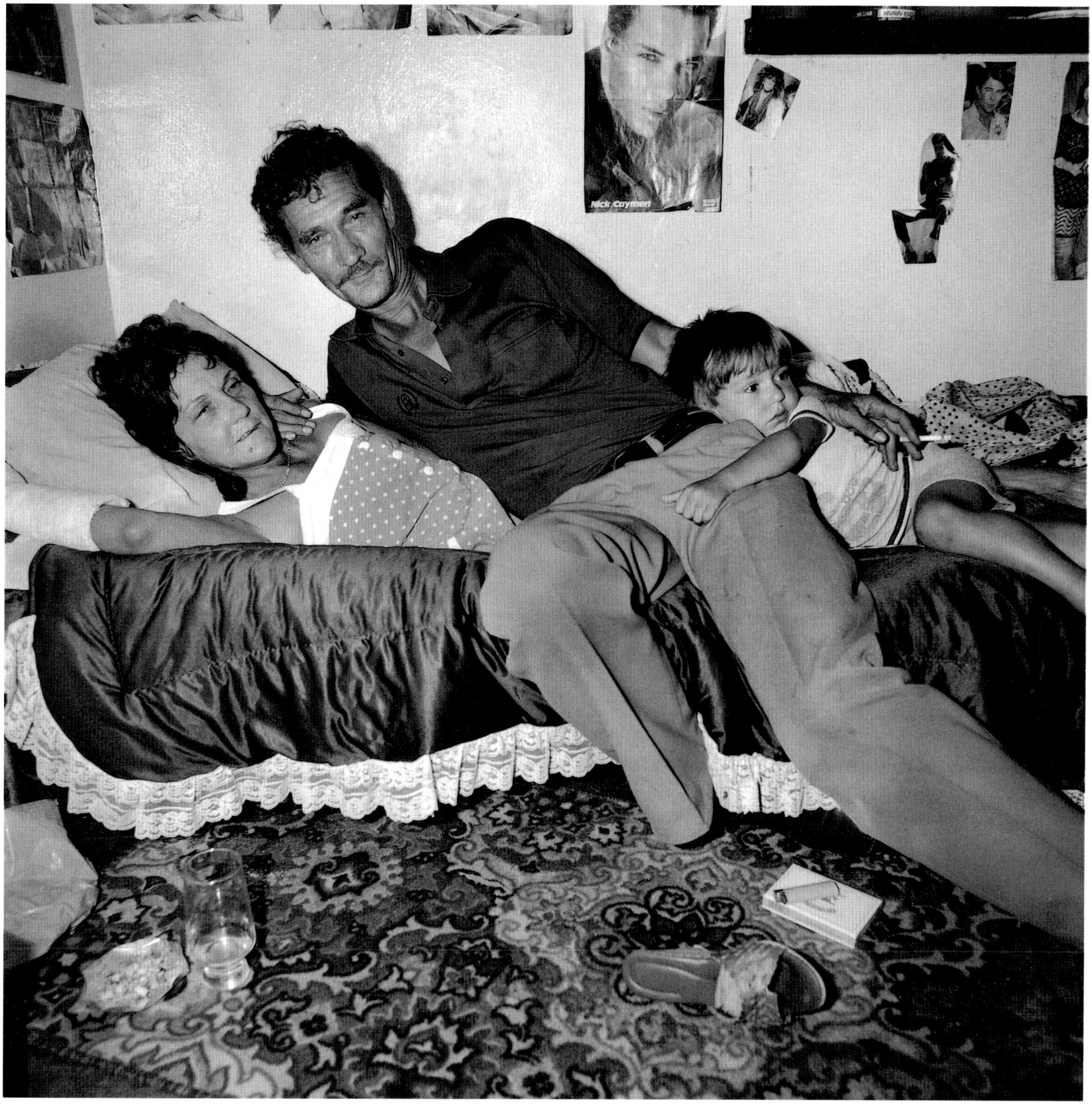
Nick Caymen

Diesel Mechanic with wife Dorothea and son Frikkie,
Central Cape, 1990

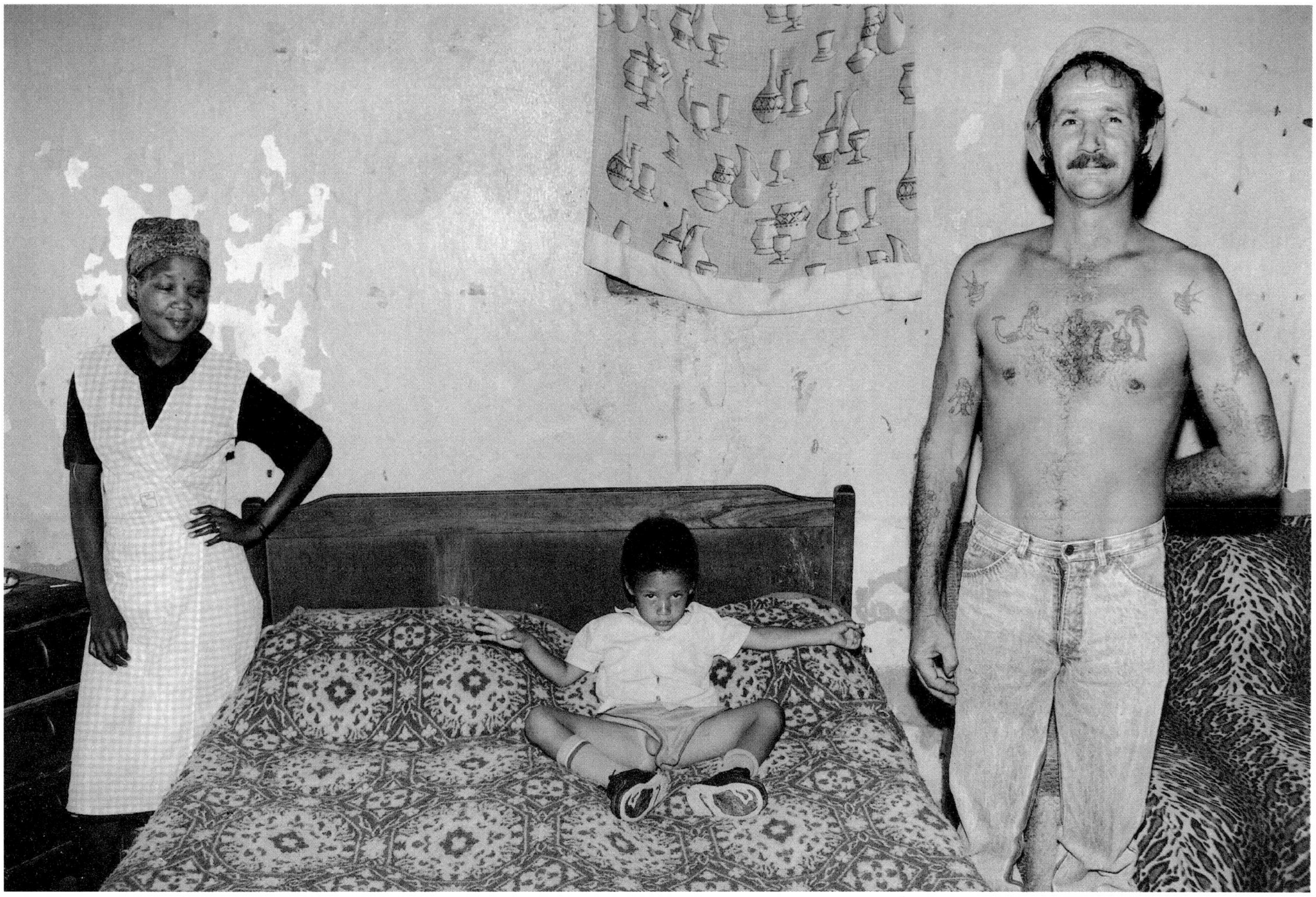

Children from circus family, Southern Cape, 1993

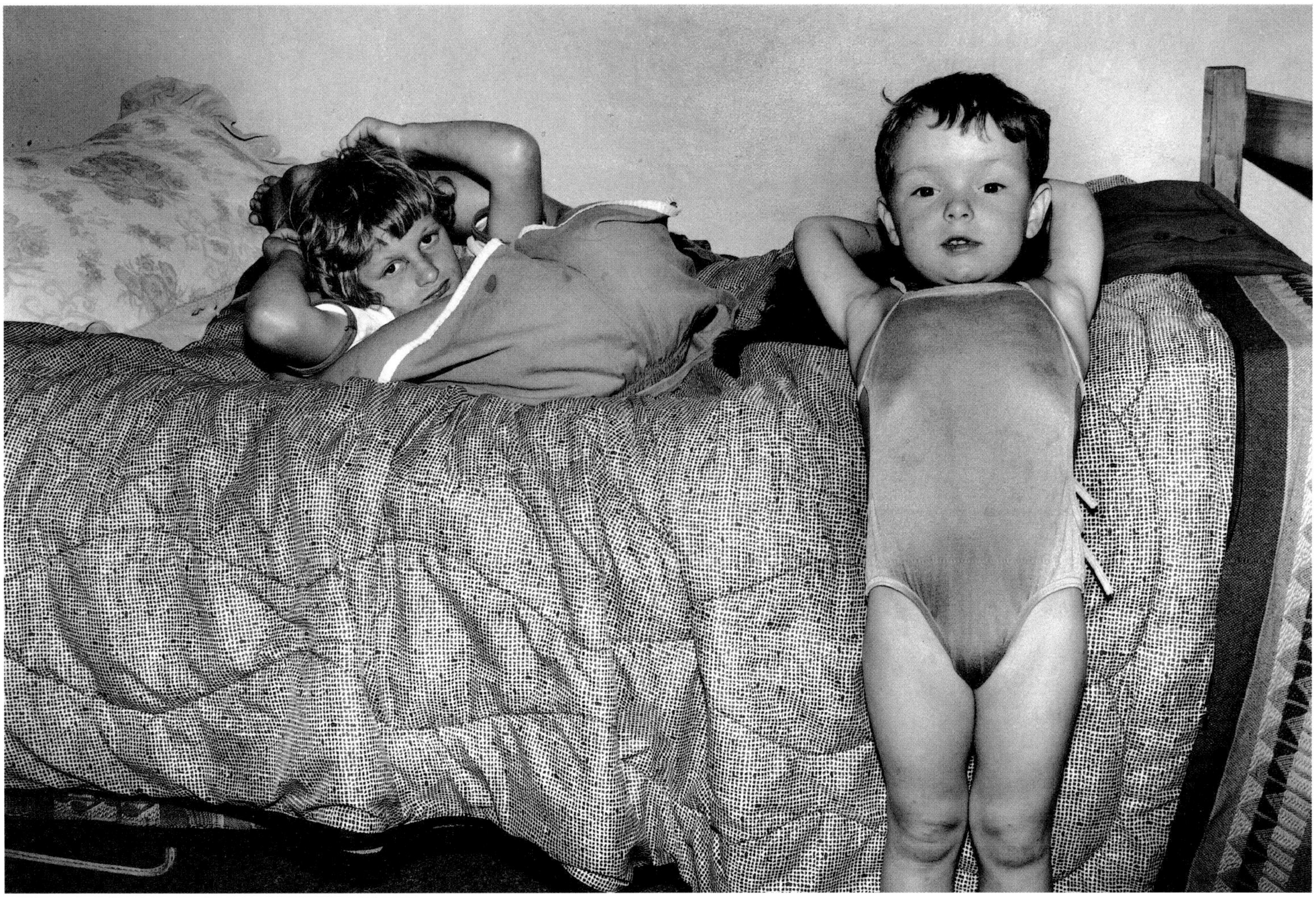

Farm worker, Northern Cape, 1993

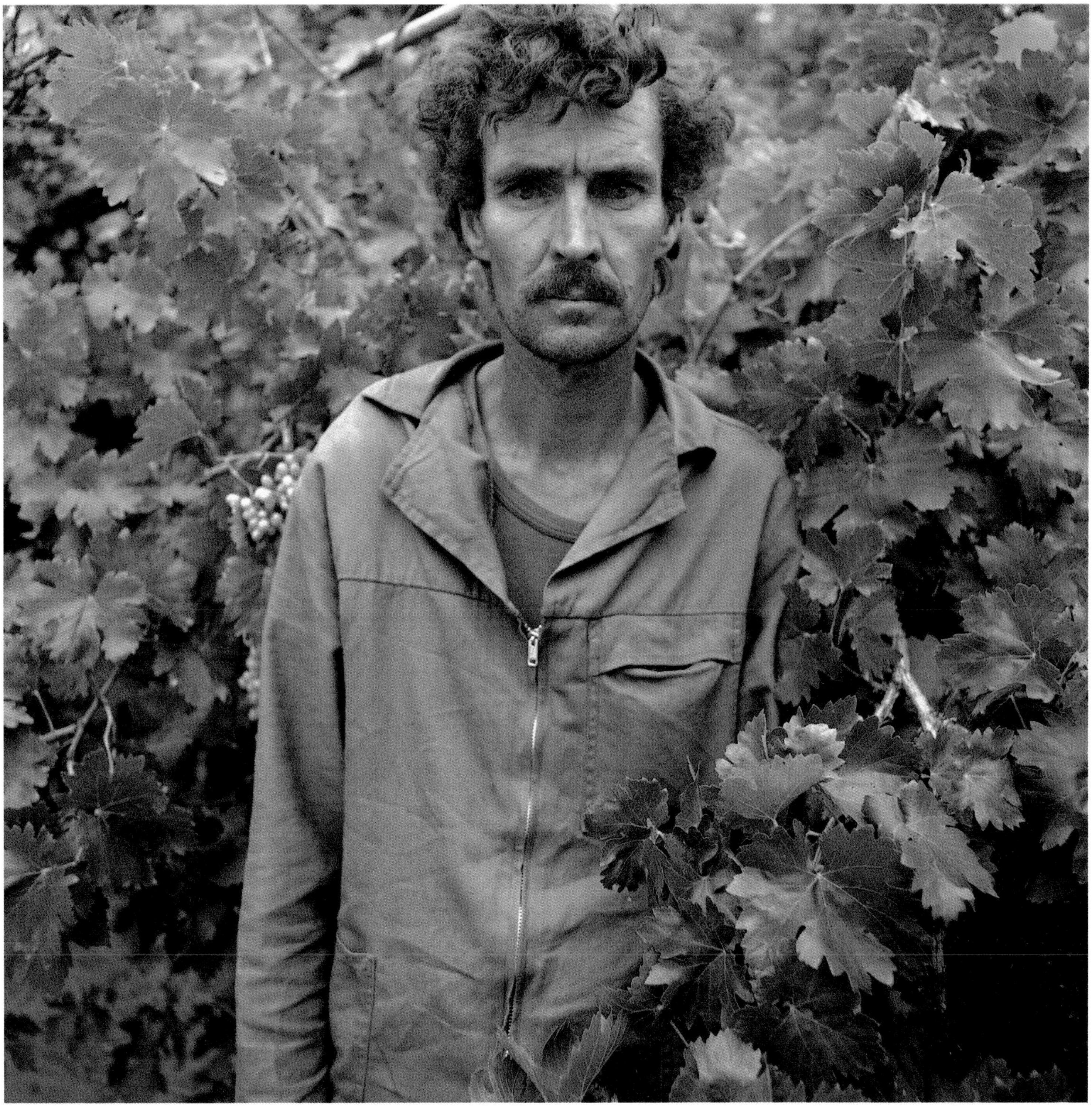

Mother and son, Orange Free State, 1993

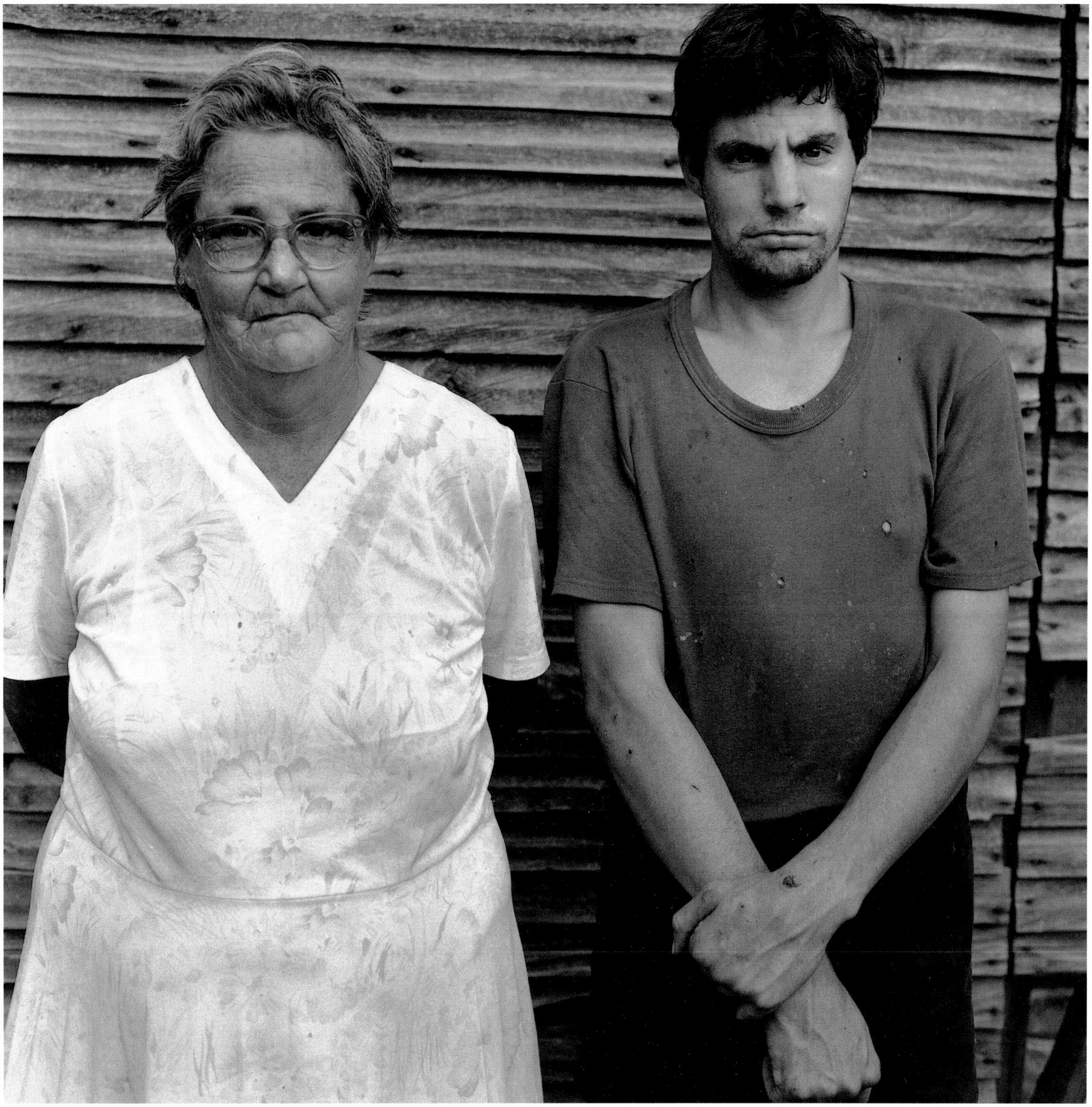

Boetie Nel, grape farmer, Northern Cape, 1990

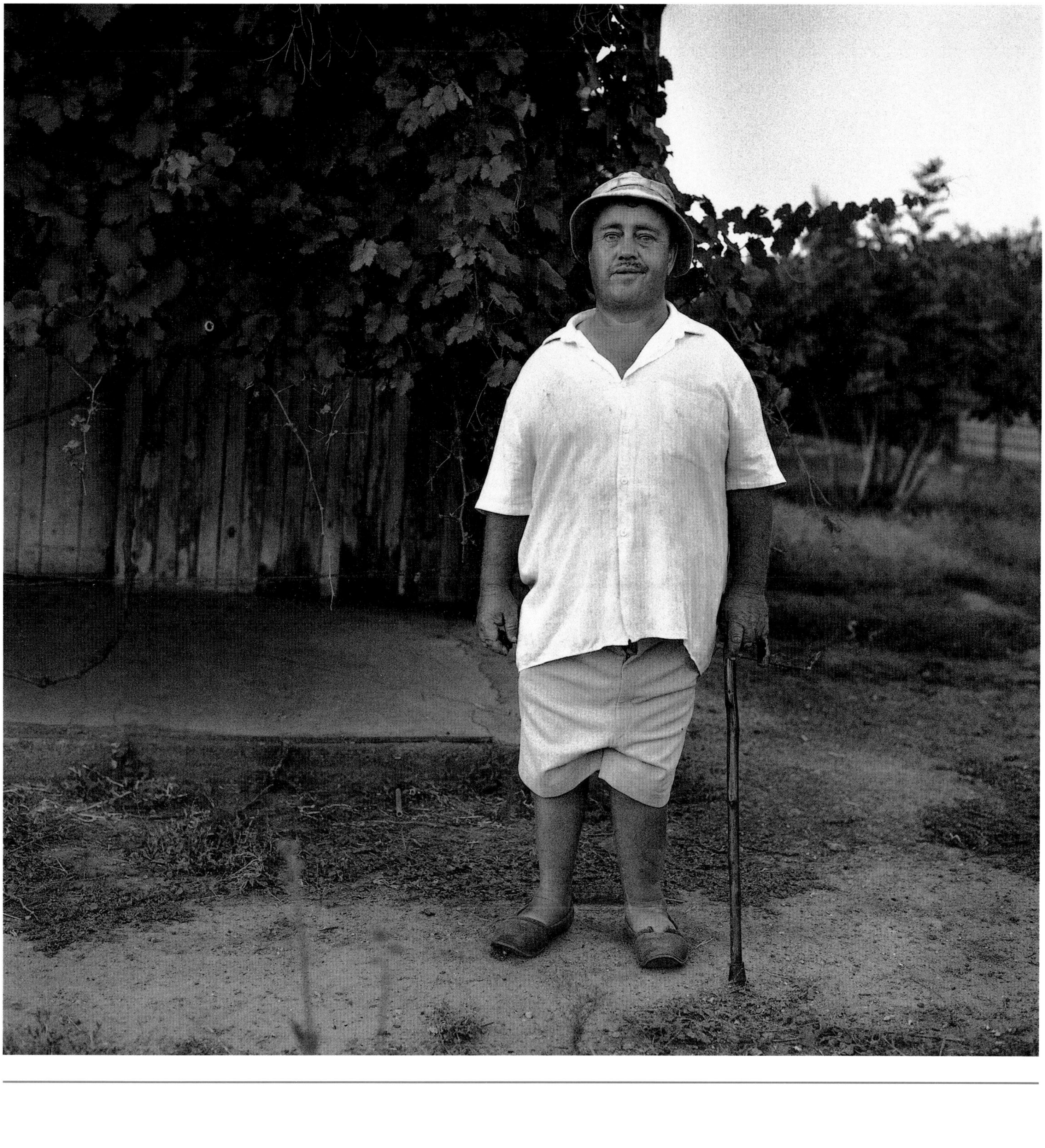

Old woman, Western Transvaal, 1992

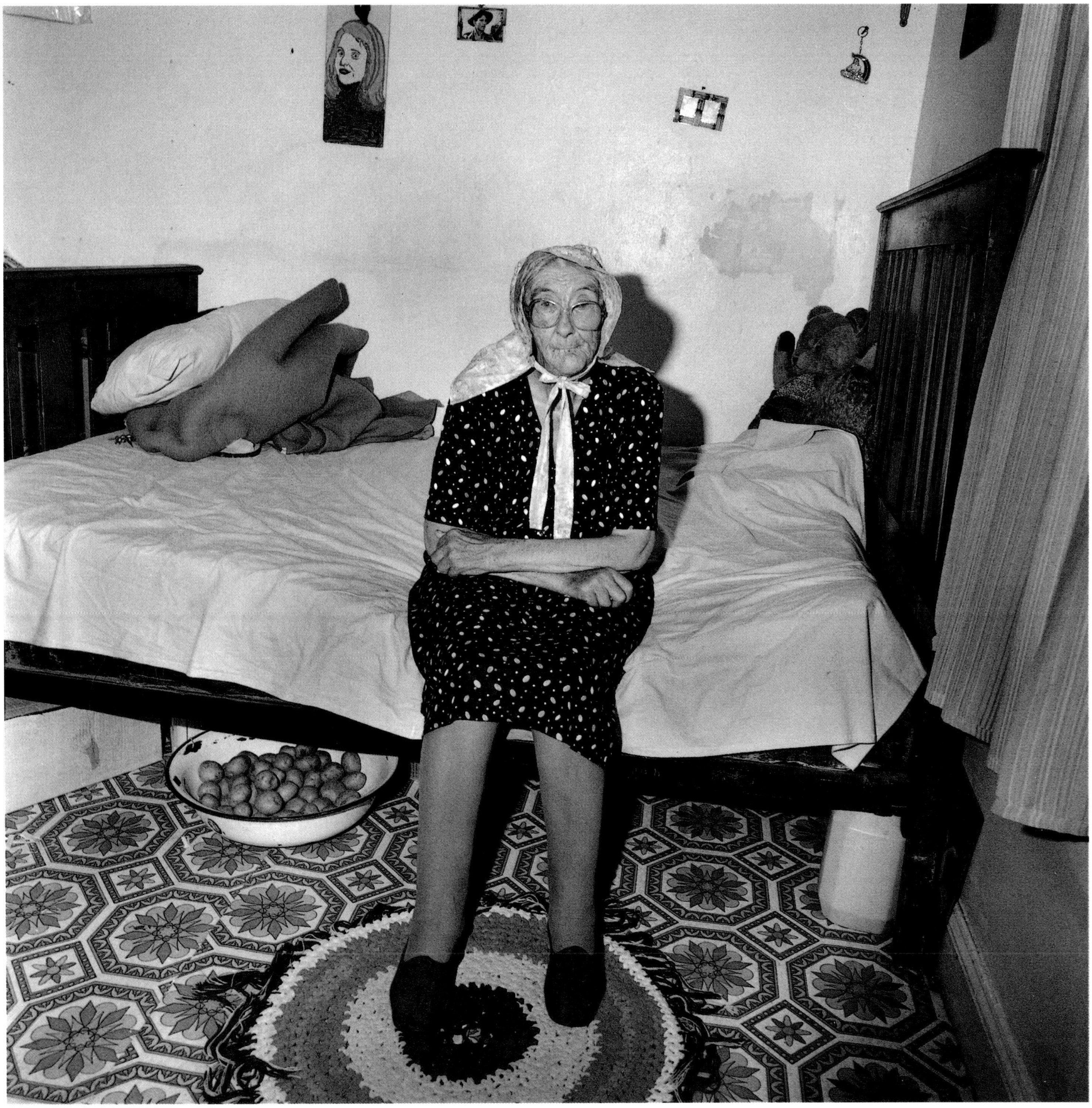

Old men, Western Transvaal, 1991

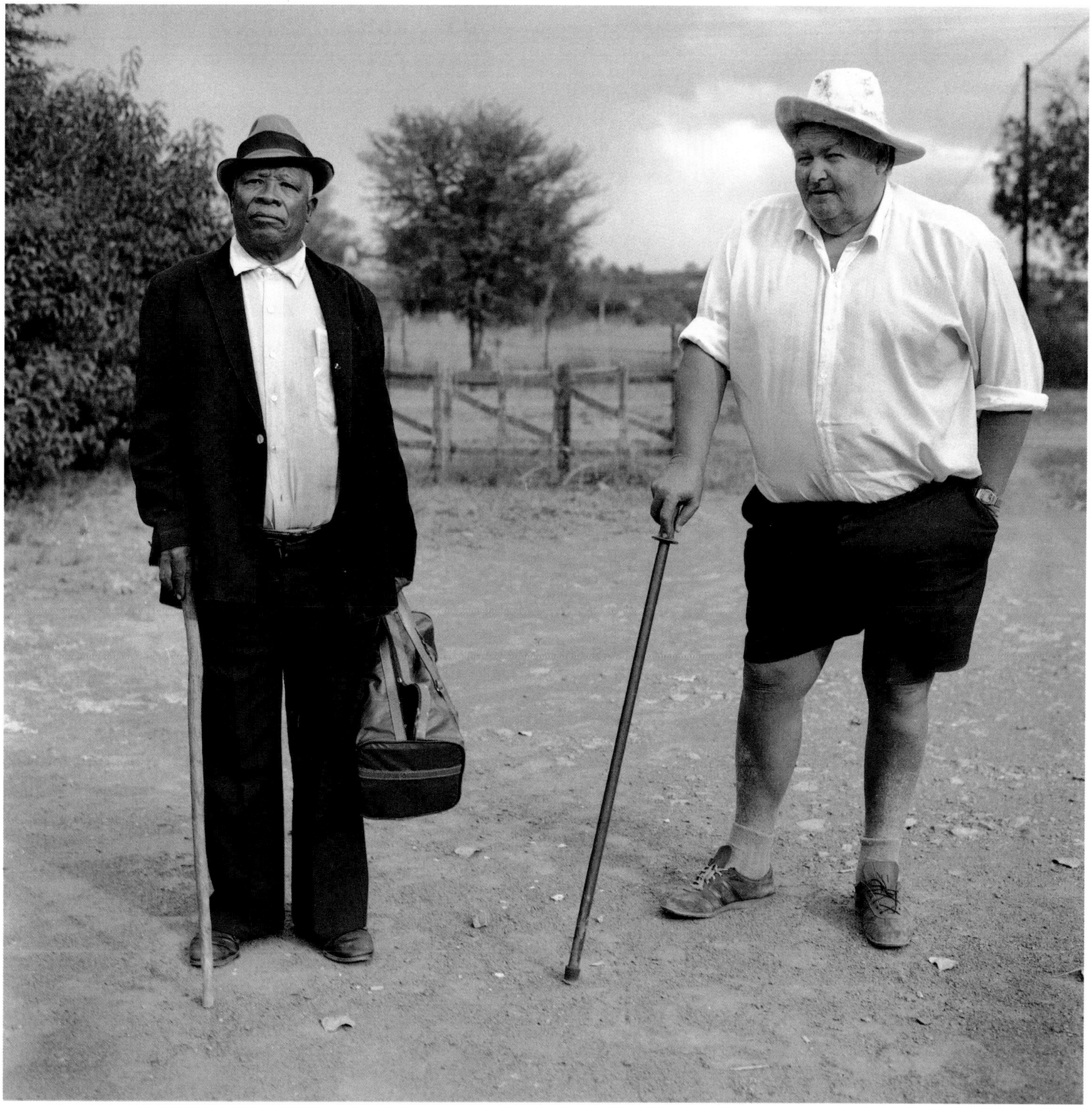